Where Will This Shoe Take You?

Also by Laurie Lawlor

Shadow Catcher: The Life and Work of Edward S. Curtis

Gold in the Hills

Where Will This Shoe Take You?

A Walk Through the History of Footwear

LAURIE LAWLOR

Walker and Company ❋ New York

For my son, John, with love.
One day, I know, he will dedicate a book to me.

First published in the United States of America in 1996 by Walker Publishing Company, Inc.

Published simultaneously in Canada by Thomas Allen & Son Canada, Limited, Markham, Ontario

Library of Congress Cataloging-in-Publication Data
Lawlor, Laurie.
Where will this shoe take you?: a walk through the history of footwear/Laurie Lawlor.
p. cm.
Includes bibliographical references and index.
Summary: A history of fashion in footwear through the ages.
ISBN 0-8027-8434-8 (hardcover). —ISBN 0-8027-8435-6 (reinforced)
1. Footwear—History—Juvenile literature. 2. Shoes—History—
Juvenile literature. 3. Fashion—History—Juvenile literature.
[1. Shoes.] I. Title.
GT2130.L35 1996
391'.413'09—dc20   96-3718
                                                    CIP
                                                    AC

Book design by Chris Welch
Printed in the United States of America
10 9 8 7 6 5 4 3 2 1

Contents

Pap made all the shoes for our big family. . . . Sometimes he didn't get to us bigger boys until purty late in the fall. I guess he thought it made us tough and healthy to go barefoot in the frost. As I was the oldest boy, it would be up toward Christmas before I got any shoes. . . . On frosty mornins in the fall we'd heat a clapboard before the fireplace until it was almost charred, stick it under our arm and run through the frost until our feet began to sting. Then we'd throw the clapboard on the ground, stood on it until our feet warmed, grab it up and make another run.

—*A Home in the Woods: Pioneer Life in Indiana*
Oliver Johnson's reminiscences of early
Marion County

*Young barefoot boys
from a small
midwestern town at the
turn of the century.*

Introduction

Shoes tell stories. In one lifetime, each of us may walk 65,000 miles—nearly two and one-half times around the world. If you carefully examine people's shoes, you can find out where they're going, where they've been. More than any other personal belonging, shoes reveal a great deal about how each of us lives, works, and plays.

In every culture around the world, what people wear (or don't wear) on their feet reflects their environment and culture and socially defined roles as men and women, adults and children. Throughout history shoes have been linked to special events—from weddings to funerals, from coronations to executions—and have served as important symbols in the traditions we celebrate and the tales we share.

Each year in the United States, more than 200,000 new footwear fashions are introduced. The same number are unveiled each year in western Europe. About half are rejected by retailers. Of the 100,000 that go into production, only about 25,000, one-eighth of the original number, will be profitable. Even so, the millions of new shoe ideas that appear on the market are based on seven old (and occasionally very ancient) shoe styles: the sandal, boot, oxford, pump, clog, mule, and moccasin.

Where will these shoes take you?

Anywhere in the world you wish!

FOOTWEAR SAYINGS

Lace into
Lay by the heels
On a shoestring
Shoestring budget
One foot in the grave
Walk a mile in his shoes
Follow in his footsteps
He's back on his feet
I have two left feet
Don't tread on me
Fast on his feet
Step right up
Heel-footed
Pussyfooting
Have cold feet
Give him a lacing
Put your foot down
Jump in with both feet
Stand on your own two feet
Getting off on the right foot
Put your foot in your mouth
Everyone on an equal footing
Can you fill his boots?
Thinking on your feet
Kick up your heels
Getting a toehold
Dancing on air

Shoe dogs
Heel and toe
Out at the heels
Take to your heels
Barefoot and pregnant
If the shoe fits, wear it
The shoes make the man
Getting your feet wet
Down at the heels
Give him the boot
Cool your heels
Foot the bill
Stepping out
Lick my boots
Head over heels
Light on your feet
You can bet your boots
Get your foot in the door
The shoe is on the other foot
Put your best foot forward
I'm glad I'm not in his shoes
To die with your boots on
Where the shoe pinches
Doing the two-step
Take it step by step
Fancy footwork
Skip to my loo

Where Will This Shoe Take You?

An Ainu girl from remote northern islands of Japan wears stockings with her sandals to keep warm.

Chapter 1

The First Shoes

Sandals and Moccasins

The foot itself is the starting point of a wonderful series of inventions.

—OTIS TUFTON MASON
PRIMITIVE TRAVEL AND TRANSPORTATION

Imagine that you don't own any shoes. Not one pair. And your two feet are your only means of transportation. What will happen when you make a run for it all the way to school? During the coldest months, your feet will probably freeze as you dash across snow and ice. Later, when summer comes and temperatures skyrocket, you'll have to highstep across blistering hot pavement, dodge broken glass and rusty nails, and somehow avoid stubbing your toes.

The fact is, we often take our shoes for granted.

Have you ever wondered who wore the first pair of

shoes and how they were invented? To start at the very beginning, we must travel back in time 100,000 years to the far southern coast of Africa. In rocky shelters and caves clustered at the mouth of the Klasies River, not far from the Indian Ocean, lived what are believed to be the first communities of *homo sapiens sapiens*. This name, which means "doubly wise man," was invented by scientists to describe the first modern humans who looked and had the capacity to think like us.

Game was plentiful along the Klasies River. Because the climate was mild, the south African settlers probably wore little clothing. They didn't need shoes. The air was warm and balmy—perfect barefoot weather.

During the next 70,000 years, however, life began to change for the early seaside *homo sapiens sapiens*. Across the globe, the climate shifted as glaciation, enormous sheets of ice, advanced and retreated. When temperatures dropped and the ice sheets expanded, sea levels fell and new coastlines appeared. In time, the Klasies River settlers found themselves no longer living directly on the coastline. Sea access was now nearly forty miles away. As herds of animals migrated to new regions in search of food, early human hunters had to migrate, too, or starve.

Their massive migration and resettlement took place over thousands and thousands of years. It required miles and miles of travel by foot in regions that varied from hot, sandy deserts and steep, rocky mountains to cold,

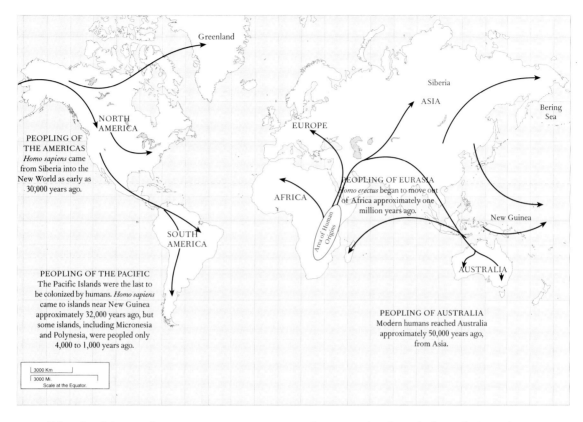

Small bands of hungry homo sapiens sapiens *may have wandered north through the Sahara Desert into northern Africa. Some continued east through Eurasia (Europe and Asia), then, possibly using simple rafts and crossing a forested land bridge with New Guinea, arrived in Australia as early as 48,000 B.C. Approximately 17,000 years later, in 31,000 B.C., early modern humans settled central Europe. Groups may have made the trek across Asia to Siberia by 28,000 B.C. Another 18,000 years passed before Asian settlers journeyed across Siberia to the Bering Sea land bridge and into North America. By 10,000 B.C. they had completed the long trip south to the far tip of South America.*

snowy tundras and wet, windy plains. To adapt to hostile environments, early humans had to come up with new ways to protect their bodies from relentless sun, snow, or rain.

They invented clothing—mostly cured animal hides. And they came up with another bright idea: shoes. The simplest, quickest way to protect the soles of the feet was to grab whatever was handy (flat chunks of bark, large leaves, perhaps bunches of grass) and tie these under the feet with vines or long tough grass. Earliest attempts at

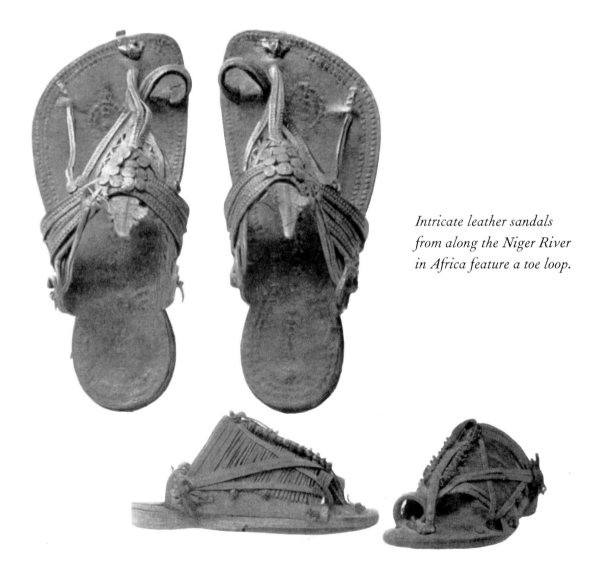

Intricate leather sandals from along the Niger River in Africa feature a toe loop.

shoes probably weren't very attractive, but they were practical.

Then after years of experimentation, someone invented sandals. Considered the oldest form of crafted footwear, early sandals were made in two basic forms. The first was created with woven palm, papyrus, or grass and attached to the foot with plant fiber loops that hooked around the toes. Ancient examples of this type of sandal have been found everywhere from Japan and parts of Polynesia to North America, among the Klamath Indians, the Ute, and prehistoric rock dwellers who once lived in what is now Arizona.

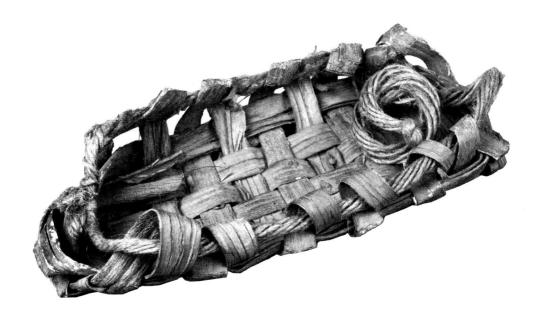

Simple Chinese sandals of woven bark have hemp rope laces threaded through a series of loops along the perimeter to keep the sandals on the feet.

The second type of early sandal was cut from treated hide, pierced with holes around the edges, and laced with a leather strap that acted as a drawstring to hold the sandal in place. One of the earliest sandals of this kind was uncovered in a mummy's grave at Pachacamac, Peru, high in the Andes Mountains. Estimated to be nearly 1,000 years old, this sandal was made of llama skin. While still wet, the skin was probably formed around the foot and bent over the toe, heel, and sides of the foot a few inches. When the skin dried, holes were punched around the edge and a drawstring strap was woven through. Sandals of the same design are still used thousands of miles away in Iceland, among the Caucasus Mountains between the Black and Caspian Seas in Asia, and in the Baltic provinces of eastern Europe!

How could the same sandal be found in such far-flung places? Some anthropologists believe that as primitive men and women traveled and settled in all corners of the globe, they copied ways of making shoes from other

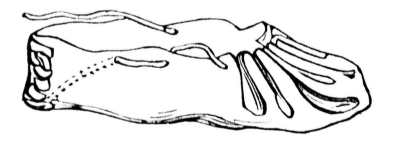

An early sandal design found in Pachacamac, Peru.

people they encountered. As ideas spread, improvements were made in borrowed designs depending on what raw materials were available and what kind of weather was experienced as seasons changed.

Scientists may never know for certain exactly where

the first sandal was invented. Was it on the hot sands of the Sahara or along rocky ocean coastlines where early humans stooped at low tide to gather shellfish? Since many of the earliest sandals were made of plant material, they deteriorated rapidly once exposed to wind and weather. Leather or hide sandals remained intact only if they had the good fortune to be dropped in a bog or lost in a salt mine. As a result, few ancient examples of ordinary people's sandals have survived long enough for archaeologists to dig them up and calculate their age with much certainty.

Where else can we look for sandal clues?

Interestingly enough, one of the oldest pictures of sandals is also the oldest known example of Egyptian writing. This 5,000-year-old carved piece of slate was discovered in Egypt in the temple of Hierakonpolis, "the city of hawks." One side of the slate shows the king punishing a hapless, kneeling enemy. The other side shows him striding barefoot past ten headless bodies. Shadowing the king wherever he goes is a dwarf-sized servant cradling the king's fancy sandals in his hands. Do the sandals represent King Narmer's special power? Perhaps.

During the next 1,500 years, Egyptians elaborated their special form of writing called hieroglyphs, which were created from drawings of human heads, animals, plants—even flowers. In 1,334 B.C., a nine-year-old boy named Tutankhamen became the Egyptian king. By this

Originally designed as a palette, a special surface to hold paint, this Egyptian carving may have been used by an Egyptian priest to touch up the eye of a temple god. Look between the two horned heads to see King Narmer's name symbolized by a fish (Nar) and a chisel (Mer).

time, the word for "sandal" had its own hieroglyph, which looked like this: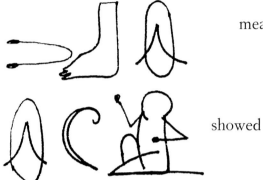

  meant "to be shod"

showed "sandal maker"

When King Tutankhamen died at age eighteen, he was mummified and buried in a magnificent tomb. A variety of splendid 3,000-year-old sandals were discovered among the clothing, food, weapons, and tools buried by his subjects, who believed these items would aid the king on his after-life journey. One pair of royal peaked, pointed sandals was fashioned from embossed gold. Another was made of papyrus, a fibrous plant used for making paper. The papyrus sandals featured leather ankle straps edged with gold ribbon and decorated with a fanciful Nile River scene that included small ducks poking their heads out of golden lotus flowers.

Sandal making in Egypt was big business. Workshops were often large and employed many people. Egyptian sandal makers, who served the wealthy and powerful, enjoyed positions of respect in their communities. To

compete with other sandal makers, they sometimes created catchy new sandals.

One enterprising sandal maker lined footwear with linen painted with a picture of the customer's enemy tied up like a slave. Hieroglyphs inside each sandal promised, "You have trodden the impure Gentiles under your

According to this wall painting from the tomb of Rekhmira, Egyptian sandal makers used their teeth to draw the straps through holes before securing the straps with knots.

feet." Another sandal maker specially arranged studs on the soles of courtesan's sandals so that their footprints would leave behind the message "Follow me."

While the rich and famous roamed ancient Egypt in fancy sandals with slogans, what were common people wearing in colder climates farther north?

After 8000 B.C., primitive hunters roamed what is now eastern Spain. When they weren't chasing stags to eat or struggling to keep warm, these early Europeans painted the walls of caves and the undersides of cliffs with

To pursue swift stags in eastern Spain, a hunter is shown in a cave painting dashing over rough terrain in boots.

pictures of men and women hunting, fighting, dancing—even climbing trees. Some of these paintings remain and show people wearing fur or skin boots.

Other early shoe evidence was discovered accidentally, high in the Tyrolean Alps on the Austrian-Italian border. In 1991 hikers stumbled upon the frozen but nearly perfectly preserved body of a 5,300-year-old man. The ancient mummy wore cold-weather, mountain-climbing gear: a fur hat that fastened under the chin, a cape made of grass or reeds, a deerskin coat, a leather loincloth, skin leggings—and on his feet, calfskin shoes filled with grass to ward off the cold. The Ice Man's shoes were held in place with braided strings.

Who may have traveled in this high, rugged altitude before the Ice Man? How did they survive? Some

Like the Ice Man, this 500-year-old mummy, which is considered to be among the oldest and best records of early Inuit life, was preserved with the help of cold and low humidity. This mummy and seven others were uncovered at a formal burial site in Qilakitisoq, Greenland, in 1975. Each of the six women and two children had been carefully dressed in warm clothing and sealskin kamiks, *or boots, for their journey to the Land of the Dead. The* kamiks *were meticulously sewn with separate soles, similar to sandals with skin stockings attached.*

anthropologists believe that the earliest travelers to make this trip may have brought their sandals with them from warmer climates. As the weather became colder, they probably pulled on "socks" to wear with their sandals. These socks or stockings were nothing like those we know today. Made of strips of leather or cloth, they were wrapped around the foot to keep it warm while the sandal provided covering for the sole.

As humans hunting animals in winter ventured into deeper snow, they may have discovered something

A picture drawn on the wall of a cave in South Africa of a bowman who may be wearing shoes.

A painting from a cave in Spain of an archer who appears to be wearing boots was made with pigments mixed from water, diluted blood, melted honey, albumen, and vegetable juice. The figure is no bigger than a human hand.

important. If they made their sandals wider and larger, they could actually walk along the snow's surface without sinking. Eureka! The first snowshoes.

One theory says that as humans traveled farther north and east from Europe into the colder climates of Asia, they may have developed special "skin stockings" to wear with snowshoes. (No one can successfully wear a snowshoe with a hard-soled shoe.) Eventually, these skin stockings became shoes that could be worn after the snowshoes were slipped off. Travelers from Asia who crossed the Bering Strait 12,000 years ago may have brought this new kind of footwear with them to North America. "Moccasin," derived from eastern Algonquin dialect, appeared for the first time in print when John Smith published his inventive "Map of Virginia" in 1612. The name has since been used to describe all different kinds of Native American shoes.

$\mathcal{S}$lip your feet into these soft moose-skin moccasins. Lift the ankle flaps and tie the bands to keep your feet snug. Where will these shoes take you?

Up the wild Yukon River to the Ingalik village of Anvik in southwestern Alaska. Here, more than 100 years ago, a group of North Athapaskan hunters, fishermen, and their families braved long, snowy winters. In summer, they faced hordes of biting flies and mosquitoes. Footwear had to provide insulation against the cold, yet remain flexible and comfortable. These moccasins did the job.

Making and repairing moccasins took much skill and time. One pair might last several months during regular use. But on a long journey over rough, wet ground, Ingalik travelers wore out as many as four or five pairs in one day. The job of making and repairing moccasins was handled entirely by women. Training started early. By age eight, most girls were helping their mothers scrape, soak, and stretch moose skin. Next, the skin was suspended in the smoke of a small wood fire to create a rich brown color. A one-piece pattern was cut from the skin using a stone knife. Holes were punched with a piece of sharpened beaver bone, and caribou sinew was drawn through to sew the moccasin pieces together. Beaver quills, which had been dyed purple with berries and yellow with ocher, were secured with sinew as decoration.

Described by one nineteenth-century visitor as "the pride of the Indian wardrobe," Northern Athapaskan moccasins were often true works of art. Sometimes the moccasins were given away as signs of friendship. Other times they were traded for food or other goods. To create beautiful moccasins required hours of practice. Mothers made their daughters take apart and redo their first moccasins again and again until they were perfect. During a special puberty ritual, girls were isolated from the rest of the village for more than a month. During this time, they sewed countless moccasins for their relatives and friends. A girl skilled in making moccasins always had plenty of offers for marriage.

Northern Athapaskan moccasins of moose hide.

Who created this particular pair of moccasins? No one knows for certain. The woman—young or old—who made them never could have guessed the long journey they would one day make. In 1893 this pair traveled thousands of miles to Chicago. The moccasins appeared in a special display at the World's Columbian Exposition, where they were admired by countless visitors from around the world.

Today's popular military boots were originally created for paratroopers during World War II.

Shoes and Protection

From Boots to Clogs

A soldier in shoes is only a soldier; but in boots, he becomes a warrior.

—GENERAL GEORGE S. PATTON
(NICKNAMED OLD BLOOD AND GUTS)

Throughout history, soldiers have used boots to protect their feet and legs. Boots for campaigns through rough country. Boots for wading across icy rivers. Boots for long treks on horseback. Little wonder, perhaps, that one of the earliest records of this type of footwear is found on the 2,700-year-old palace mural of King Sargon II (721–705 B.C.), a military mastermind who ruthlessly spearheaded the expansion of the Assyrian empire that would one day stretch from the Persian Gulf to the Mediterranean. The mural's stone carving captures forever King Sargon II's warriors—swift

A military horseman wearing laced boots, is pictured wading through a river in this Assyrian alabaster relief from the palace of Sanherib (705–680 B.C.) in Nineveh.

horsemen in chariots, fierce infantry, and deadly archers—all wearing snug-fitting leather boots that laced from knee to instep.

Unlike the camouflage boots of later generations of soldiers, Assyrian boots were often colorfully decorated with bright embroidery and glinting bronze or brass ornaments. Spartan soldiers of ancient Greece hundreds of years later would sport even flashier footwear—brilliant red leather boots (and matching red tunics) designed to conceal blood flowing from wounds. When red boots became the rage among war-mad Spartan youth, officials quickly put an end to the fad. Only soldiers going to war, they said, were allowed to wear red boots.

Some historians are convinced that boots date back further than ancient Greece and Assyria. Perhaps 4,500 years ago, boots may have been first developed as moccasins with separate wraparound leggings to ward off the cold and protect the legs from prickly underbrush. Eventually, the leggings were attached to the moccasins, creating boots that reached to the midcalf or knee. Not surprisingly, this type of boot has been found extensively in northern Asia, where the climate is hostile. Experts think that many of these early boots were brought across the Bering Strait to Alaska and the rest of North America and adapted by Inuit and Native American tribes.

Like other shoes, boot designs change depending on the needs and the available resources of the people making and wearing them. Animals have often provided boot inspiration. When Inuit living above the Arctic circle noticed that polar bear skin did not freeze even in the coldest temperatures, they created boots using the complete leg skin and paw of the giant bear (claws included). The Ainu, aboriginal people of the North

An early-nineteenth-century woodcut shows a woman from Greenland in midcalf boots.

In 1654, a Danish expedition to Greenland captured these four Inuit, who were brought to Norway and painted by an unknown artist before being taken to Denmark. The Inuit women, who prepared and sewed the over-sized, watertight sealskin kamiks *shown, later died of typhus in Copenhagen.*

Pacific living on Hakkaido, the northernmost island of Japan, made boots with the complete leg skins of deer.

Inhabitants of Nunivak Island off the coast of Alaska found that skins of caribou and bearded seal made the best winter boots. The leg hide of caribou was used for boot tops while waterproof soles were cut from old kayak covers of bearded seal. The soles were then sewn to the boot tops.

For the best waterproof boots, Inuit and Samoyed people used sealskin with the hair on the outside. Hip-

An Inuit woman in remote northwestern Canada preparing sealskins used to make boots. All skins had to be chewed soft to break the fibers.

Fish skin was sometimes used to create shoes, as in these beaded moccasins from Greenland.

length sealskin boots were worn when tending seal and fishing nets. Oddly enough, skins of salmon, pike, and burbot weren't much good as boots in wet conditions. The Kamchadal, who lived in the far eastern peninsula of Kamchatka in Russia, experienced harsh winters with severe winds and heavy snows. Summers were cool and foggy. The Kamchadal claimed that fish-skin boots worked fine in frost but were unusable in rainy weather. They were handy, however, during famines, when they could be quickly boiled and eaten.

Missing Socks

*A*mong polar Eskimos in Alaska and Samoyed tribes in the far northern reaches of Siberia, dry feet could mean the difference between life and death. The Eskimo used two layers of grass and socks made of bird skin. The Samoyed wrapped their feet in dried grass. Next came a layer of hare skin, then an inner boot, then more grass, and finally the outer boot.

To keep their feet warm, Nunivak Islanders wore sealskin socks and stuffed their boots with coarse grass. The grass, which had been gathered in October, acted as a cushioned insole to absorb moisture. Every two or three days the insole was replaced with more grass. Lapps, herding people living in the northern part of Scandinavia, also used grass to keep their boots warm and dry. The Lapps cut and dried sedge grass, then combed it into fine broken strands with an iron-tooth comb. Farmers in Sweden, Finland, and Norway copied the practice.

Socks have been made out of everything from puppy skins to woven grass. The reindeer-hide sock (upper right) with the fur outside was worn inside winter boots by Alaskan Eskimos near the Bering Strait. Such heavy socks didn't need to be worn with rain boots (upper left) or summer boots (bottom).

Bootlegs and Baby Carriers

*T*wo hundred years ago, British pirates and some members of the early American merchant navy wore high boots with broad tops that were convenient for "bootlegging," or smuggling valuables. ("Bootlegging" later became a popular term in America during Prohibition in the 1920s, when bootleggers illegally produced and sold liquor.)

Eskimo women living on the Arctic coast west of Greenland more than two centuries ago found another practical (and legal) use for their enormous reindeer-skin boots. They used them as a handy way to tote their babies. "The mothers took their children from their wide boots where they usually carry them naked," reported Sir John Franklin (1786–1847), an Englishman who led a 5,500-mile exploring expedition from Hudson Bay to the Arctic in 1819.

By 1909, Greenland women, here in their summer camp near Egedesminde, Greenland, were carrying their babies on their backs inside their hoods, instead of inside their enormous boots.

Today men and women sport every kind of cowboy boot, from fancy, plum-colored lizard boots with bulldogged heels to those with flying-eagle inlaid uppers, even though they may never ride anything wilder than the subway.

Traditionally, boots have provided protection for horseback riders who spend long days in the saddle. The American cowboy boot developed in the United States around 1867, when the first enormous cattle drives began up the Chisolm Trail from Texas to Abilene, Kansas.

The earliest cowboy boots, influenced by the riding gear of the Mexican *vaquero,* were created by bootmakers in Kansas. These plain black or dark brown cowhide boots weren't fancy, but they were practical. Their narrow toes slipped easily into stirrups. When the cowboy stood up in the saddle to rope a steer, the reinforced steel arches helped brace his feet. If the cowboy's horse stopped or turned unexpectedly, high, underslung heels helped his feet stay in place in the stirrups. Tall boot tops helped protect against chafing from the horse and injury from brushes with cactus and rattlesnakes. Spurs were attached to the heels with a crescent-shaped piece of leather that hooked over the instep. While spurs helped prod the horse to gallop, they served no real purpose while the cowboy walked about town, except to announce his presence with a loud, satisfying jangling.

The era of long cattle drives lasted only twenty years—from 1867 to 1887—but the popularity of cowboy boots grew throughout the twentieth century.

A New Pair of Shoes

The Shoemaker by David Teniers (1610–1690) shows the shoemaker at work. Only 100 years ago, most people purchased shoes from a similar small, stuffy shop that smelled of tanned leather. The shoemaker, wearing an apron, sat on a bench or low stool surrounded by tools: hammer, leather-cutting moon knife, awl, and nipper to remove nails and old soles. Wooden lasts (forms used to shape

the upper part of the shoe) came in various sizes. The customer was fitted for new shoes by standing in stocking feet on a piece of paper while the shoemaker made an outline in pencil. It took a month for a pair to be made by hand. These were called "straights"—no right or left.

Only the very wealthy could afford to have servants "break in" their new shoes by wearing them for six months so that they finally became comfortable. Everyone else had to suffer through blisters, bunions, and chafed ankles and toes. As this early nineteenth-century English etching shows: "New boots—Confound the fellow—never shall get them off! They squeeze my feet to a Jelly!"

What are some other shoes that have kept people's feet safe and sound on the job? For more than 2,000 years, wooden clogs and wooden-soled shoes have provided affordable protection for men and women working in mills, mines, quarries, farms, docks, and laundries around the world. The Dutch call them *klompen,* the Germans *die panpoffel* or *die Holzschuh* (literally, the wooden shoe), and the French *sabots.* Among early Romans, they were named *gallicae* after the rainy, cold country of the Gauls. The English based the name they gave them (clogs) on an old word meaning "lump of wood."

Long ago, craftsmen known as bodgers cut and stacked to dry rough blocks of alder, pine, walnut, or beechwood. Clog makers then shaped as many as six pairs of clogs a day using a hatchet, a hammer, and a special knife with a curved blade. Many clog makers had their own distinctive toe shapes: some upturned, others duck-billed or a narrow square.

Clogs have served other purposes besides sturdy protection. During the early days of the Industrial Revolution in Europe, French and Belgian workers protested job layoffs by throwing their sabots into the machinery and causing factory shutdowns. Out of the clog-inspired chaos, a new word was created: sabotage.

Breton peasants in France worked together to create wooden sabots.

$\mathcal{S}$lide your feet inside these wooden clogs. Where will they take you?

To the Netherlands, one hundred years ago.

The first thing you'd notice if you took a few steps was that you must rock forward in a special rolling motion to keep moving along smoothly. Wooden clogs were heavier than leather shoes. If your clogs were too big, beware. Your friends might call you a "clonk-clomper."

What was the trick to keeping clogs on your feet? Thick, itchy wool socks. To keep new stockings from wearing out at the heels, mothers coated them with melted pitch, then dipped them in turf ashes to reinforce the weaving. To make sure your feet stayed warm during the coldest months, you could line the inside of your clogs with crackling bits of hay or dried bracken (ferns).

As you and your friends walked along the cobblestone

A handy hole in wooden clogs from the Netherlands helps quickly drain water that may have accumulated on boggy walks.

street, your clogs would thump, *clomp-clomp-clomp*. If your clogs were reinforced at the bottom with special iron rings to keep the heels from wearing away too quickly, you could use your clogs to "strike fire" by swiftly knocking the clog irons against the pavement curbstone.

When winter came, walking in clogs became very tricky. Snow clung to the wooden soles. With every step, your snow stilts would grow higher and higher. Watch out! The only way to get rid of the snow (known in England as "clog-gins," "clog-balls," "snowbogs," or "cloggybogs") was to knock your foot against the curb. (Perhaps your friends preferred to annoy the neighbors by tapping their snowy clogs against the walls of houses!)

Another way to amuse yourself in winter was to skate along icy patches in your clogs. All you needed to do was bend your ankles and throw your weight on the outside edge of the clog, and off you'd go!

Clogs came in especially handy on December 5, St. Nicholas Eve. That night, clogs were stuffed with a carrot or some straw for St. Nicholas's great white horse and a poem for the bearded gentleman himself and left beside the sitting-room fireplace. In the morning (if you had been very good), you might discover that your wooden shoes had been emptied and refilled by Sinterklaas (Santa Claus) with treats—chocolate, toys, or perhaps nugget-shaped, spice-filled cookies called *pepernoten*.

Louis XIV in his red high-heeled shoes, from an etching by Antoine Masson, 1697.

Chapter 3

Shoes and Authority

What the Leaders Wore

> The wearing of shoes . . . was seen as an effort to establish relationships . . . between the ruled and their rulers. [In nineteenth-century India] Indians were always forced to remove their shoes or sandals when entering British . . . offices and homes. On the other hand, the British always insisted on wearing shoes when entering Indian spaces, including mosques and temples.
>
> —BERNARD S. COHN
> *THE INVENTION OF TRADITION*
> "REPRESENTING AUTHORITY IN
> VICTORIAN INDIA"

King Louis XIV of France stood just five feet three inches in his stocking feet. In spite of his small size, he had big ideas. The Sun King, as he was called, ruled longer than practically any other king in Europe—from 1643 to 1715. He led France's army in four major wars with almost every country in Europe. He built a glittering pleasure palace and garden known as Versailles. Despite these accomplishments, he wasn't satisfied. He still wished to dazzle the world as a glorious, invincible, magnificent, *tall* monarch.

To solve his height problem, he wore a towering wig

and high-heeled shoes. On special public occasions, he slipped into five-inch heels made of cork that were decorated with miniature paintings of victorious French battles (mostly his). Sometimes his heels displayed gentler scenes—lovely shepherdesses and flowers. Most often, the heels were covered in leather dyed red, the color that came to symbolize membership in the nobility.

Like Louis XIV's red heels, shoe color has often symbolized power. In A.D. 800, Charlemagne (also known as Charles the Great) was crowned Emperor of the Holy Roman Empire by Pope Leo III—after conquering most of Europe. Charlemagne wore incredible red leather shoes bedecked with gold and emeralds to match his jeweled crown.

Purple was another royal shoe color. During the early days of the Roman empire, only the emperor was allowed to wear the *tzanga*, a purple leather sandal embroidered with gold thread and finished with a golden eagle over the instep. Anyone who dared wear the same special shoe would be exiled and lose all worldly goods, according to Roman law. On special occasions, nobility and patricians were allowed to be seen in snug-fitting, ankle-high purple boots.

Some Roman rulers were very fussy about their subjects' shoe color and decoration. Emperor Aurelian (A.D. 212–275) proclaimed that no other man except himself and his successors could wear red shoes. Emperor Heliogabalus (A.D. 205–222) forbade all

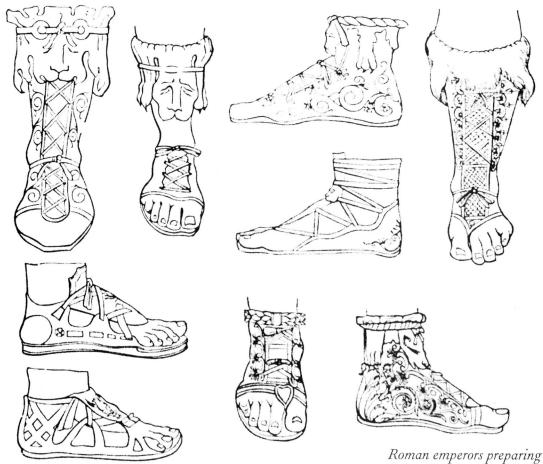

women except those of the highest ranks of nobility to embellish their shoes with gold and jewels. Poppaea Sabina, the second wife of infamous Roman emperor Nero (A.D. 37–68), ordered shoes made of pure gold. Unfortunately, her cruel husband's silver shoes were her undoing. He reportedly used them to kick her to death.

Roman emperors preparing for battle donned ornate purple sandals called the campagus, *elegant pearl- and gem-encrusted footwear (upper left) that laced up to the knee, decorated with a small animal's skin, including muzzle and paws. The finishing touch—gold nails studding the soles.*

Shoes not only can reveal political status, they can also say a great deal about a leader's philosophy about government. Thomas Jefferson (1743–1826), who assumed office as the third president of the United States in 1801, later said he wished his tombstone to read: "Author of the Declaration of Independence, Author of the Statute of Virginia for Religious Freedom and Father of the University of Virginia—and not a word more." Among the many accomplishments he failed to mention were architect, naturalist, linguist—and the first president to wear oxford shoes with shoelaces.

While low-cut shoe boots called oxfords had been introduced by students at Oxford University in England as early as 1640, shoelaces were still very new—and caused something of a stir, especially when worn by the president at a fancy reception. The *New York Evening Post* described Jefferson "dressed in his suit of customary black, with shoes that laced tight round the ankle and closed with a neat leathern string." Shoelaces! "A foppish follower of Parisian fads," the newspaper declared. What was wrong with the customary silver buckles every other distinguished man in America wore?

Jefferson undoubtedly did not mean to be a trendsetter. He was simply inspired by the new revolutionary spirit he had witnessed in France while serving as U.S. minister from 1785 to 1789. Frenchmen had given up silver buckles for shoelaces, which they considered more "democratic." Jefferson simply meant to do the same.

Thomas Jefferson in oxfords with "foppish" French shoelaces.

Unfortunately, his symbolic use of shoes—and shoelaces—backfired, because Americans did not understand their French meaning.

Military boots have also been used as symbols. When Napoleon I (1769–1821) of France seized power and crowned himself emperor in 1804 in a ceremony presided over by Pope Pius VII, he started a whole new trend in footwear. Considered one of the most brilliant military figures in history, Napoleon was a great admirer of the arts and costume of imperial Rome. His favorite black leather boots rose up over the knees in front but were cut away in the back for ease of movement. To maintain the necessary shine, Napoleon's boots required hours of labor with special oils and wax mixtures. Not one dull spot was allowed.

Just as sports stars' victories today are celebrated with sales of team shirts, people one hundred years ago celebrated military victory by copying the winning general's shoe style.

The British victory over Napoleon in 1815 at the Battle of Waterloo was engineered by Arthur Wellesley, the greatly admired first Duke of Wellington (1769–1852). (Wellington once admitted that he owed his military success to the fact that his soldiers were "the best shod in Europe.") Like Napoleon, Wellington was a big fan of boots. Wellingtons, as they were later named, were "leg boots," snug-fitting boots that rose to the knee. Wellington could never have predicted the popularity of his boot style, which was quickly adopted by both soldiers and gentlemen, who wished to stay as far away from dangerous battlefields as possible.

Two military boots, the Wellington (right) and the black leather Hessian (left), were favorites even among those who never marched to war during the nineteenth century. One upper-class dandy from England named Beau Brummell insisted his valet shine his boots with a secret ingredient: champagne.

$\mathcal{P}$ull on these enormous boots. Where will they take you?

To Washington, D.C., more than 130 years ago.

The fancy black leather dress boots were reportedly worn by President Abraham Lincoln on April 14, 1865, the night he was assassinated while attending a play at the Ford Theater.

At six feet four inches, Lincoln towered over most men of his day. A British visitor in 1861 described the president as "a tall, lank, lean man . . . with stooping shoulders, long pendulous arms, terminating in hands of extraordinary dimensions, which, however, were far exceeded in proportion by his feet."

Lincoln's feet—measuring size fourteen—were very big for his day. Because Lincoln was flat-footed and slightly pigeon-toed, he was plagued with aching corns and bunions most of his adult life. No wonder he eagerly shucked off his boots when he worked at the White House. His habit of flip-flopping about in carpet slippers astonished visiting dignitaries, who could not imagine the chief executive going bootless. Even Mrs. Lincoln's nagging had no effect. It wasn't long before some wags in Washington dubbed Lincoln "Diplomat in Carpet Slippers."

In 1864, Lincoln met an ambitious Pennsylvania shoe-

After Lincoln was shot on April 14, 1865, at Ford's Theater, he was taken across the street to a boardinghouse to be tended by doctors. After he had died, these boots were reportedly removed and left behind in a closet. Later, a boarder found them and sold the Lincoln relics to grubstake a claim out West.

maker named Peter Kahler, who promised he could solve the president's foot problems. Kahler visited the White House on December 13, 1864. While Lincoln stood in his stockings on a sheet of plain brown paper, the genial German immigrant traced the outlines of his feet in ink. Lincoln signed and dated the piece of paper. In March 1865, Kahler sent to the White House a pair of French calfskin boots for the president and a complimentary pair of slippers for the first lady. (Surely Mary Todd Lincoln never wore them in public.)

Peter Kahler, an ambitious German immigrant shoe-maker, went to the White House to draw this outline of Lincoln's enormous feet on a "big sheet of thick, brown paper."

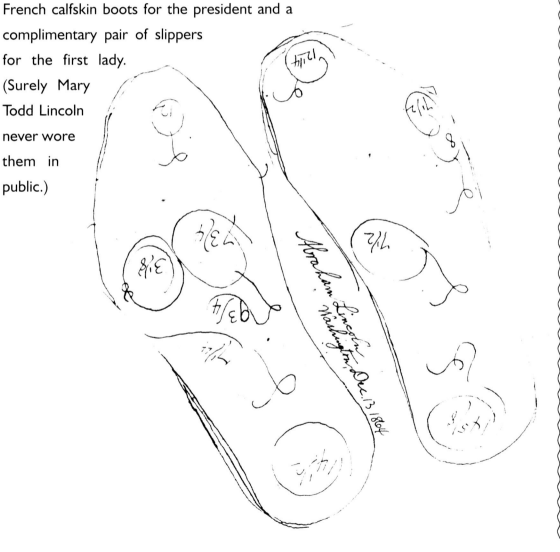

Six weeks later, Lincoln was dead. His accomplishments, his memory, and his boots remain.

Shortly after his funeral, another tale about Lincoln and his footwear circulated in Washington. The story said that Senator Charles Sumner of Massachusetts once discovered Lincoln at the White House shining a pair of boots. "Why, Mr. President," the shocked senator asked, "do you black your own boots?"

"Whose boots did you think I blacked?" Lincoln was said to have replied.

President Lincoln (and his young son Tad) posed for a photograph at the Gardner Studio in Washington, D.C., in 1865 wearing the fine calfskin boots made by Kahler.

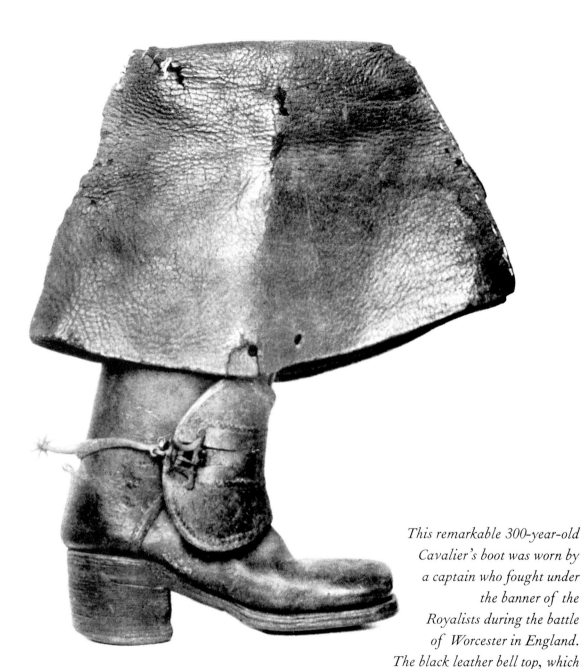

This remarkable 300-year-old
Cavalier's boot was worn by
a captain who fought under
the banner of the
Royalists during the battle
of Worcester in England.
The black leather bell top, which
measures ten inches across, could be pulled up over the knee and thigh.
The boot's heel, composed of thirteen layers of leather, is two and
one-half inches high.

Chapter 4

Shoes and Status

From Bare Feet to Bound Feet

> He treated his boots, misshapen, broken and elderly as they
> were, with the reverence and love of a peasant who knows
> that without them he is finished: no credibility, no mobility
> and above all, no work.
>
> —COLIN MCDOWELL
> *SHOES: FASHION AND FANTASY*

In ancient Greece, shoes signified the difference between slavery and freedom. "Bare feet," wrote Greek philosopher Plutarch (c. A.D. 46–120), "a sign of slave's degradation." Slaves were not allowed to wear shoes except in the country, when they could wear thick wooden-soled sandals. When slaves were sold, their bare feet were covered with chalk or plaster. As a result, they were called *cretati*, "chalk people." No free Greek would dare be seen in public without his shoes for fear of being mistaken for a slave.

Historically, shoes have revealed wealth and could be

Poor field-workers often go barefoot. In contrast, the wealthy vie for status with outrageously expensive footwear. The most expensive on record? A pearl-studded pair of shoes created in Paris in 1977 for the self-coronation of Emperor Field Marshal Jean Fedor Bokassa of Central African Empire. The cost: eighty-five thousand dollars.

used to identify an individual's social status, politics—even religion. For example, an English girl who wore ox-hide shoes 270 years ago was considered very different from a young lady who sported laced shoes with high heels—even if her fine boots were hand-me-downs from the "missus" for whom she worked.

For poor and working-class people around the world, shoes have often been an unaffordable luxury. In 1748, English workmen's shoes were studded with heavy hobnails in the sole and metal "horseshoes" at the heels so that the shoes would last as long as possible. And little wonder. A pair of shoes at the time cost a workman nearly half a month's wages. (Translated into compara-

In 1638, Elias Holl the Younger sketched this peasant, who depended on having boots to do field work and stay alive. Almost 300 years later, Louis Hughes, a Tennessee slave, recalled the importance of shoes in his own survival:

"For winter the men had each two pairs of pants, one coat, one hat and one pair of coarse shoes. These shoes before being worn had to be greased with tallow, with a little tar in it. It was always a happy time when the men got these winter goods—it brought many a smile to their faces, though the supply was meager and the articles of the cheapest."

ble modern terms, this would place the price tag of a pair of shoes at approximately $1,000.)

Not surprisingly, donating brand-new shoes to the needy was considered an uncommonly generous gesture. Six hundred years ago, John Rychard, "burgess of town of Bristol" in England, promised in his will dated "23 Marche, 1411": "I bequeath to 24 poor persons on the day of my burial 24 pair of shoes." Another wealthy citizen, a "clothier of London" named Bartholomew Neve, vowed on March 3, 1401, that when he died his

A seventeenth-century French aristocrat once owned these high-heeled pointed shoes of white goatskin embroidered in silk.

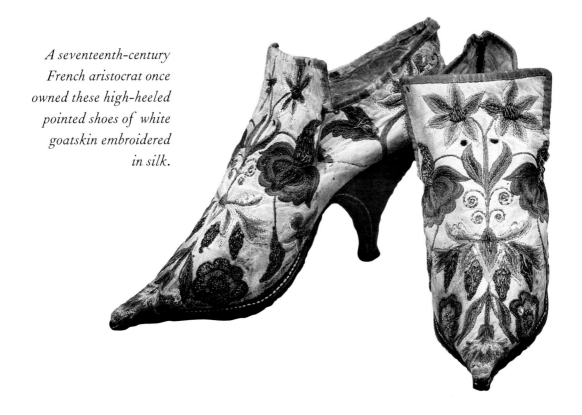

The Difference Between Us

*I*n *The Age of Indiscretion*, Clyde Davis recalled growing up in a small town in Missouri at the turn of the century:

> The most curious difference in clothing between us of the elite and the Highview children was in footgear. In the winter we wore shoes that were bought for us individually. They wore no shoes even in winter months except in very cold or slushy weather. Then the Highview boys and girls alike wore women's shoes—high button shoes usually—that turned up at the toes like the strange old-time slippers of court jesters or Persian potentates. It was very funny indeed to see a tough Highview boy hobbling along through the slush in a pair of suede-top high-heeled female shoes, and you could yell at him, "Hey, Snotty, where you get the shoes?" provided of course, that you had your gang with you and he didn't have his gang with him.

heirs would give "to each leper living in 'les Meselcotes' of Holborn, one pair of shoes."

For the very wealthy, there have been few limits as to the number of shoes they might acquire for themselves. Empress Elizabeth (1709–62) assumed the throne in 1741 and ruled Russia for twenty years. When she died, she had accumulated more than 15,000 dresses and thousands of matching pairs of shoes and slippers—all of which had to be carefully maintained by servants. The sixth, last, and only wife to survive English king Henry

VIII was Catherine Parr (1512–48). In 1543, the year Catherine was married, she immediately purchased forty-seven pairs of shoes. (Her speedy shopping may have been a good idea, considering how quickly the king beheaded some of his other wives.)

Throughout history, ownership of certain shoe styles has identified membership in the wealthiest class. Named for the Polish city of Kracow, the "crackow" was a pointed or "snouted" shoe with a curled tip worn by men in Europe in the fourteenth century. Made of leather or velvet, the crackow (also called a poulaine) became longer and longer until the toes had to be stuffed with hay, wool, or moss and shaped with whalebone to keep the tip standing upright.

The longer the toe, the richer the wearer—and the more unlikely he needed to do any physical work at all. How could he? A gentleman in crackows could barely walk. He had to shuffle along in a flapping, mincing gait, almost like a dance step, to keep from falling on his face.

Under the fifty-year reign of Edward III of England

This leather crackow from the fourteenth or fifteenth century measures fifteen inches from pointed toe to heel.

Where Will This Shoe Take You?

(1327–77), new shoe rules were proclaimed. The prince could wear crackow points as long as he liked. Noblemen were limited to twenty-four inches in length, gentlemen to twelve inches, and commoners to six inches. Some upper-class men who flapped about in the style added small silver bells (aptly called "folly bells") to the tips of their shoes, which had become so long that a thin chain was suspended from the toe and connected to a garter at the knee. The melodious crackow is said to have inspired the nursery rhyme: "Ride a cock horse to Banbury Cross, to see a fine lady upon a white horse, with rings on her fingers and bells on her toes, she shall have music wherever she goes."

Not everyone was thrilled with the new style. One critic in 1362 declared, "Their shoes, which they call 'crakows,' have curved peaks more than a finger in length fastened to the knees with chains of gold and silver, resembling the claws of demons rather than ornaments for human

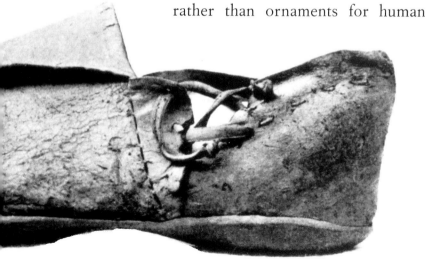

It's hard to imagine how a fifteenth-century German nobleman in full armor wearing these fashionable pointy steel sabatons *managed to mount his horse.*

beings." Even the Pope tried to ban crackows as "lewd." Eventually, this fashion of the very wealthy peaked out, and shoe toes shrank.

In addition to displaying wealth, shoes have been used to declare political affiliations. In France in the eighteenth century, high-heeled buckled shoes were the rage—until the French Revolution began in the late 1780s. When the guillotine picked up speed chopping off heads of kings, queens, and nobility left and right, the wealthy who managed to survive began to wonder whether wearing conspicuous diamond shoe buckles was worth risking their necks. From that point on, less expensive footwear and shoe fasteners became the style. Politically correct shoes were flat, heelless, and fastened with simple shoestrings or patriotic red, white, and blue ribbons. Some wealthy women adopted the "democratic look" by draping themselves in Greek togas and donning simple sandals. (Never mind the diamonds decorating their toes.)

Four hundred years ago, Puritan men in Holland proclaimed their no-nonsense politics by wearing tall black hats banded with a matching plain leather strap, dull-colored coats, and plain, blunt, square-toed shoes. In 1649, Cavaliers in England who opposed severe Oliver Cromwell

A seventeenth-century
Puritan in traditional dress.

(1599–1658), showed their protest with a completely different look: long curly hair, beribboned clothes, silk hose, and high-heeled, swashbuckling, bucket-top boots trimmed with ruffles.

Shoes have also served as another very different kind of symbol. For many, what was worn on the feet signified religious affiliation. Three hundred years ago in Turkey, pious followers of Muhammad wore yellow boots and slippers to show their devotion as Muslims. In the mountainous country of Tibet, *lamas*, or monks, could be distinguished not only by their shaved heads but by their bright red cloth or wool boots with brocaded decoration around the ankles and upturned toes called "sledge runners." The soles of lamas' colorful Tibetan boots were often made of yak hide.

Sumptuary Law

$\mathcal{T}$he New World offered a new beginning for many who fled England's oppressive social system, religious persecution, and economic depression in the 1600s. The colony of Virginia beckoned with limitless land, abundant streams, and forests.

As the colony prospered, some Virginians were able to afford fine clothing and shoes imported from England. Others paid Colonial shoemakers to copy the latest European styles. In 1619, the first session of the Virginia House of Burgesses tried to prevent "excess of apparel among plain people and ordered offenders be fined by local parishes." The Colonial lawmakers were outraged. Why should Colonists born as laborers "take upon them the garb of gentlemen by wearing gold or silver lace, or buttons, or points at their knees, or to walk in great boots?"

Sumptuary laws, rules that tell certain groups what they can and cannot wear, were difficult to enforce in early America. Wealth more than anything else set indi-

viduals apart. If a Colonist could afford to wear great boots and stomp about like a gentleman, who could stop him? "Nothing has ever been effective against the passion to move up in the world," wrote historian Fernand Braudel.

Three ships sailed into Chesapeake Bay, Virginia, in 1607 with 105 men who had left England to set up the first permanent colony in America. These fortune seekers wore tight-fitting, garish doublets of heavy brocade. Lace hung from their sleeves, and enormous, high-heeled boots adorned their feet. Their impractical dress was matched by their skills. Few were accustomed to hard work; not one was listed as "shoemaker."

Catholic monastic orders, such as the Capuchins and Franciscans, historically required monks to wear simple leather or wooden sandals to show their humility and "separation from worldly vanities." When some monks strayed from the dress code, a strict warning was issued in 1363 by the head of the Benedictine order. "We absolutely forbid, both for the monks and for prelates of this province, boots which are pointed [rostratas] or too narrow, together with silk girdles, or girdles of any such material, or with silver adornments, and hoods ornamented with silk or sandal of green or blue or any other color but plain black."

What is worn (or not worn) on the feet gives clues about many different religions. Early Hebrew priests did not enter temples wearing shoes, because footwear was believed to defile holy ground. Buddhist monks and nuns as well as followers of Islam have traditionally followed the same custom. Shoshone medicine men always remove their moccasins when they smoke special tobacco pipes in healing ceremonies. Pythagoras, a Greek mathematician and philosopher who lived in the sixth century B.C., was never seen without plaited papyrus sandals similar to Egyptian priests'. He refused to wear leather sandals, he said, because he did not wish to contaminate himself "with the skin of a despoiled animal."

These shoes are so small, they fit in the palm of your hand. Turn them over and look at the bottom—sky blue satin and embroidered birds and flowers. If you could put your foot in these unusual shoes, where would they take you?

To China 200 years ago. Legend says that lotus or lily foot slippers, as these were called, first appeared in China in the eleventh century when Empress Taki was born with deformed feet. So that the future empress would not feel embarrassed, her father announced to the court that only women with very small feet could be considered truly feminine and desirable. Young women of the court immediately tried to follow this new edict by binding and eventually deforming their own feet by trying to make them as small as

Chinese lily foot slippers, approximately life size.

possible. Other legends say that the tradition developed during the Sung Dynasty (A.D. 960-1279) among court dancers who had very tiny feet and performed on strewn lotus and lily blossoms.

Whatever the origin, foot binding eventually became the mark of beauty and gentility among Chinese women. The binding process began at age five or seven by the girl's mother, nurse, or older sister. The bandage, two inches wide and ten feet long, was wrapped to bend the four smaller toes inward under the foot. Eventually, the bones in the foot stopped growing, and the foot of a grown woman might be only four inches long.

Having bound feet was considered an honor and made the girl more valued as a wife. A common saying 2,000 years ago was: "A tiny foot can atone for three-quarters of a woman's ugliness." Bound feet were thought to be a sign of grace, cultural breeding, even intelligence.

Upper-class women in lily foot slippers, photographed at the turn of the century in Canton, China.

Having bound feet, however, meant a young girl could not run or jump without great difficulty. She could not work. As she grew older, her steps became tiny and delicate. She walked only with the support of a servant or a long staff to help her keep her balance. Her gait, described as "fragile as a weed in the breeze," was known as the "willow walk."

Chinese women spent many hours sewing and embroidering lotus slippers, which often seem like tiny tapestries of bright color. These were not ordinary shoes. They had no hard sole, and were often made of soft, padded upper cloth to cover the entire foot and ankle like a small baby's bootee or a doll's shoe. They were to be kept immaculately clean and were often perfumed.

The practice of binding feet in China officially ended in 1902 when an imperial decree announced that no child could have bound feet. However, the tradition persisted secretly. During the introduction of Communism in China in 1921 and the civil war that erupted in the 1930s, unbound feet proved to be politically dangerous. When armies supporting the traditional regime marched into a village, girls with unbound feet were viewed as Communist sympathizers while girls with bound feet were permitted to go free.

Today the Chinese custom no longer continues. Only the tiny slippers remain as reminders.

Rhinestone platform shoes boosted rock star Elton John's stature by five inches during his concerts in the 1970s.

Chapter 5

Shoes and Fashion

Heels and Beyond

When I've got shoes with wings on,
the town is full of rhythm and the world's in rhyme,
and living has no strings on.

—*FROM* "Shoes with Wings On"
MUSIC BY IRA GERSHWIN
LYRICS BY HARRY WARREN

Fashion is about how people feel. The shoe styles we choose communicate not only our emotions but our hopes and dreams.

In times of uncertainty and military strife, solid, no-nonsense boots often tend to be the shoes of choice. More than 300 years ago, endless war and unrest plagued Europe. The future looked very bleak. During the stormy reign of England's Charles I (1600–49), who lost his throne and was beheaded during the English Civil War, everyone from military officers to coachmen swaggered about "half-buried," one critic complained, in

"monstrous wide boots, fringed at the top."

Across the English Channel in enemy territory, every type of Frenchman was also pulling on long boots, a process that was something of a struggle. Fashionable boots had become so tight, the best-dressed gentlemen had to dip their legs in water before the boot could be put on with help from a servant.

Shoes and the Female Ideal

One hundred fifty years ago, fashionable women's shoes did not encourage women to exercise—or leave the house. Who would want to, when walking meant picking your way over lumpy cobblestone streets in thin-soled, miniature slippers that pinched your toes? Even if a fashionable woman went out in a carriage, her high-button boots with fourteen pairs of tiny eyelets took forever to fasten. Worse yet, because petite feet were considered attractive, many women squeezed their feet into shoes too narrow and too small. As a result, many walked with a mincing (undoubtedly painful) gait. "Women's shoes," one historian remarked, "helped to enforce the vision of the ideal woman as a weak sedentary creature who lived almost entirely indoors."

Napoleon's empress, Josephine of France (1763–1814), was no exception to the

Heelless, backless slippers, or mules, *richly embroidered in silk and gold thread and trimmed with ribbons and metal lace, best exemplified the protected life of the seventeenth-century English woman who wore them. Her feet must have been very small or very cramped. The slippers measure only eight and one-half inches in length.*

Fussy bustles, fancy hats, and impossibly tiny high-button boots made athletic activity impossible for young girls, shown in this 1889 issue of Supplement to Young Ladies Journal.

Twenty buttons had to be secured before the nineteenth-century woman who wore these thin-soled boots could go outdoors— preferably on a very short walk in good weather.

The latest style in shoes, portrayed here, prompted fiery Englishwoman Frances Milton Trollope (1780–1863) to comment: "[Fashionable American women] . . . walk in the middle of winter with their poor little toes pinched into a miniature slipper, incapable of excluding as much moisture as might bedew a primrose."

early-nineteenth-century ideal. Once, she reportedly returned a brand-new pair of delicate slippers to the shoemaker after discovering a small hole.

"Ah, I see your problem," the shoemaker replied. "Madame, you have walked in them."

Not until 1850 did it become socially acceptable for women to participate in outdoor sports: croquet (1860), tennis (1870), hiking (1880), and bicycling (1890). By 1900, outdoor exercise was "considered absolutely necessary to a woman's health and appearance." Shoes changed, too—slowly but surely. The December 1860 *Godey's Lady's Book* was able to report: "From Mr. Bowden of the shoe department, we learn that thick walking boots for ladies are universal this winter, and no one will be required by elegance or fashion to shiver along in thin soles."

Fashionable women everywhere must have been greatly relieved.

Who begins shoe fashions? Many years ago, it might have been kings or queens and other people of influence. In the 1600s, Charles II (1630–85) was dubbed the Merry Monarch—"the cleverest and laziest of English kings." Charles II, who enjoyed horse racing, gambling, and the jovial company of pretty women, wore silk roses attached to the tops of his blunt-toed shoes. Other wealthy men and women in court quickly copied the Merry Monarch's style, each trying to outdo the next in magnificence and color.

Sometimes shoe fashion was copied by the wealthiest or most powerful from styles already worn by members of the working class. Pumps were first described in England in 1555 as "thin shoes . . . not fastened on with lachettes, but lyke [sic] a poumpe [sic] close about the foote." They were low-cut shoes with cork or leather soles designed for running footmen who had to jog alongside their master's carriage to be ready to open the door when the vehicle stopped. By 1730, the young, rich, and restless had taken over the style, modified now with velvet.

The invention of the heel caused one of the most dramatic fashion changes. Originally, heels may have been inspired by a very practical need to keep the hems of skirts out of rain, mud, and snow. Women in the Near East had already discovered *chopines* perhaps 500 years ago. Chopines worn by women in Turkey were like miniature stilts, eight inches high, made of wood, and inlaid with mother-of-pearl and silver wire. Bands of leather formed sandal-like straps that went around the foot.

So many women began wearing chopines in Venice, Italy, in the sixteenth century, one visitor complained that it seemed as if the country was populated by "walking maypoles." Wealthy women in Venice, a city of canals and boats, seldom walked anywhere. If they had to walk, they needed assistance from a servant at each elbow so they wouldn't topple over. Soon, the fashion spread to France and England, where chopines grew as high as eighteen inches!

Three hundred years ago, the woman who wore these cork chopines covered in white leather added a whopping seven and one-half inches to her height.

The stiltlike shoes never caught on completely. During the early part of the 1500s, an anonymous Italian shoe designer came up with an ingenious solution: height without the chopine's awkwardness. When Catherine de' Medici (1519–89) sailed from Italy to marry the Duke of Orleans, she brought along something special in her baggage: the first high-heeled shoes to be seen in France. Cork wedges were attached to the front of the sole with a higher section in the back under

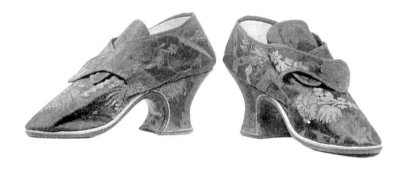

Dainty eighteenth-century lady's shoes from England (top) feature bright yellow brocade heels nearly three inches tall. This extraordinary shoe for an eighteenth-century Englishman allowed him to boost his height a full six inches. Unfortunately, he probably wasn't able to walk without a cane.

the heel to give savvy Catherine the height she needed to look her future husband, who would one day be King Henry II, straight in the eye.

High-heeled shoes quickly became the rage, mandating that shoemakers now create different shoe soles for left and right feet (not just "straights" as they were called). At first, the new heels made of cork or wood—rising three, four, even five inches—made the wearer's legs swell with discomfort. Women teetered about in a puppetlike, stilted gait to keep from falling over. The French called the new heeled footwear *chaussure à port*, or bridge shoes (because of the arch), and *chaussure à cric*, or clicking shoes (because of the sound they made).

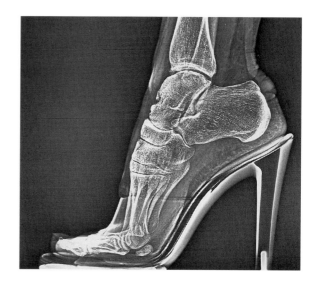

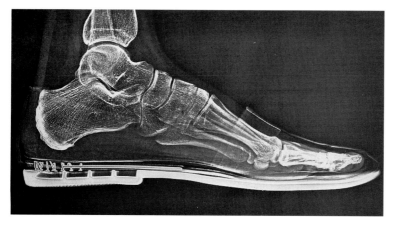

The 52 bones in your feet comprise nearly one-quarter of all the bones in your body. X rays reveal the effect of fashionable high heels (above) on the foot compared with low heels (left).

Architecture and Shoes

Shoe fashion echoes architecture. During Henry VIII's reign (1509–47), English houses and churches were built with massive facades designed with horizontal lines and broad surfaces broken only with symmetrically placed windows and doors. During this same era, Henry VIII and his court began wearing broad, robust shoes with rounded broad toes.

Two hundred years earlier, cathedrals with soaring steeples had emerged all over Europe. Women's clothes reflected the new Gothic building style: tall, pointed headdresses, long, slender cuffs to their sleeves, long tails on hoods, and very pointed shoes. Stained-glass windows adorned cathedrals, and shoes took up the style. To imitate the colorful windows, shoemakers slashed the tops of shoes so that many different layers of bright fabric would show through.

The peaked shoe, or crackow, the "steeple head-dress," and the cathedral spire of the fourteenth century all emerged around the same time in Europe.

Fashion Time Capsule

If ever in some centuries to come, the long-toed shoe[s]
of the modern fine Gentlemen should be discovered in some
Museum of Antiquities, they would no doubt give birth
to many learned doubts and speculations.

—THE *TIMES*

LONDON, SEPTEMBER 20, 1799

*Y*ears ago, fashions changed much more slowly than they do today. Improved communication, television, movies, newspapers, and magazines relay the latest styles from one corner of the globe to the next with amazing speed.

And yet some things never change.

Shoe fashions now as in years past echo styles in clothing. First, the fashion is worn by trendsetters. Long ago, these may have been kings, queens, and their court. Today, trendsetters might be movie stars, rock stars, or fashion models. When a large group of people copy the style, it truly becomes "the fashion." Finally, the style becomes more and more exaggerated, ridiculous, and uncomfortable, and begins to decline.

Then the cycle repeats itself—only this time with a new shoe fashion.

Years and years from now, what will people think when they examine shoes from the twentieth and twenty-first centuries? Here is just a sampling of what they might uncover.

*Modern colorful polyurethane clogs—
practical, durable, and more lightweight
than their wooden predecessors.*

Sandals that promise a foot massage.

In 1940, the original suede Buc was introduced by G. H. Bass, which expanded the look into a line of wing-tip oxfords.

In 1963 a fashionable leather school shoe for children sported a turned-up toe.

High-fashion heels of the 1990s.

The oxford has become a standard men's dress and business shoe.

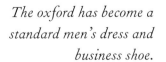

$\mathcal{T}$uck your feet into these shoes. Where will they take you?

To faraway Japan, 200 years ago.

If you wore *geta* sandals like this, you'd have to walk carefully to keep your balance. *Clip-clop, clip-clop, clip-clop.* The wooden platform sandals sang as you hurried along the crowded streets of the ancient city of Kyoto. Watch out for that puddle! The two-inch-tall getas helped keep the hem of your long kimono out of puddles—as well as mud and snow. The traditional Japanese kimono, worn by men and women, boys and girls, was wrapped, draped, and tied at the waist. One kimono alone required a twenty-foot length of silk! Since you might have worn many different colored kimonos at one time, getas came in handy to keep your clothing clean.

When you arrived home, you had to be sure to slip off

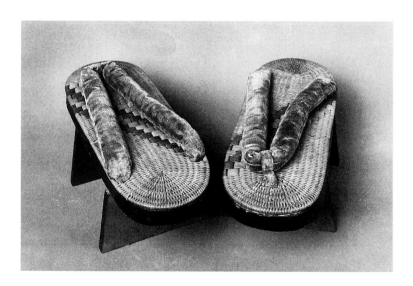

Geta *sandals from Japan.*

your getas before opening the sliding rice-paper door and coming inside. Getas, considered unclean outdoor shoes, were never worn indoors. When you took off your getas and stepped indoors onto a tatami mat that covered the floor, your feet wouldn't be cold. You'd be wearing snug cotton socks called *tabi,* specially designed for thongs so that you could still wiggle your big toe.

When it was time to go outdoors again, you'd find your getas waiting with others beside the door. Big getas, little getas. Some were carved from cedar. Others were made from oak, pine, or light *kiri* wood. While the geta's basic shape remained the same, men traditionally wore gray, black, or brown thongs while women wore green. In very rainy weather, caps of lacquered leather, oil cloth, or paper were fastened over the front of the geta and held at the heel by cords to help keep toes dry.

The exalted emperor wore the most magnificent getas of all. These were called *koma-getas.* The wooden base appeared to be one solid piece, but it was actually hollow. Komo-getas were painted with shiny black lacquer and stood nearly a foot tall. Emperor Meiji (1852–1912) at his coronation wore komo-getas of wood covered in velvet. Emperor Hirohito (1901–89) took the throne in 1926 wearing carved wooden komo-getas covered with silk.

"You ought to be ashamed of yourself," says Dorothy to the
Cowardly Lion in L. Frank Baum's Wonderful Wizard of Oz
(1900), illustrated by W. W. Denslow.

Chapter 6

Shoes and Magic

Myth and Literature

Dorothy now took Toto up solemnly in her arms, and having said one last good-by she clapped the heels of her shoes together three times.

"Take me home to Aunt Em!"

Instantly she was whirling through the air, so swiftly that all she could see or feel was the wind whistling past her ears.

—L. Frank Baum
The Wizard of Oz

In the summer of 1899, L. Frank Baum sat on the porch of a summer cottage in Michigan with an unlit cigar in his mouth. He pecked away at a noisy manual type-writer, copying page after page from his longhand man-uscript—a stack of stationery, wrapping paper, and pa-per scraps. Baum probably didn't smell the Lake Michigan breeze or hear the chickadees in the pines. He was far away in a land called Oz.

His book for children, originally named *The Wonderful Wizard of Oz*, would one day be called the first American fairy tale. And why not? It had all the

Dorothy's slippers became ruby colored in 1939 when MGM released The Wizard of Oz *in Technicolor.*

trappings of a classic: wicked witches, talking scarecrows, flying monkeys—and, of course, magic slippers. The slippers were essential in helping Dorothy fly home to her family in Kansas. Dorothy's slippers were originally silver in Baum's book, published in 1900. Metro Goldwyn Mayer insisted on changing them to ruby slippers when *The Wizard of Oz* was released as a movie in 1939. Why? The studio wanted to show off its latest innovation—Technicolor.

Health and Healing

*I*n Holland, shoe magic was once considered so potent, tradition said that if a man was struck by lightning, his relatives had to bury all his shoes as quickly as possible so that supernatural forces would not spread.

In Colonial America, the remedy for a stomachache was to lie on the floor and place heavy boots on the abdomen. Ancient Greeks claimed the best remedy for a stomachache was to eat the tongue of an old leather shoe. To aid digestion, Mongolians simply removed their shoes.

Folk wisdom from the African country of Madagascar said that wearing monkey-skin sandals would cure almost any ailment. Monkey skin wasn't easily available in Europe during the fourteenth century when bubonic plague wiped out an estimated 75 million people. In desperation, many Londoners fled the city and hurried to tanneries where shoe leather was cured. They believed that sniffing the strong smell of the tanneries would protect them from the dreaded Black Death.

In some parts of the world, shoes have protected the health and safety of individuals. Italian mothers have been known to tie red bows on their children's shoes to "avert the evil eye." Old shoes of a lost child in rural Ireland were supposedly buried to enable the child to be found. The Inuit of Greenland wore miniature soles of reindeer hide *kamiks* or boots around their necks to ensure a safe journey and warm, dry feet.

A custom in China says that buying and wearing new shoes for the New Year's celebration will bring good luck. Likewise, an ancient Roman belief assured good luck for the person who put their right shoe on first every morning and always entered a building with the right foot first. Perhaps that explains the origin of the expression "Getting off on the right foot."

Feathers and Footprints

On the windblown, treeless plains of western Australia, aborigines created slippers called *karara*. Resembling messy bird nests, the slippers were in fact carefully constructed from a combination of human hair and the brownish gray feathers of the giant emu, a five-foot-tall native bird.

Traditionally, feathers have been used to gain assistance from divine or supernatural powers. Among the aborigines, a medicine man had special connections to the spirit world. The karara were used by medicine men in secret revenge rituals, known as *kurdaitcha,* to avenge a tribesman's death.

Some experts believe that feather slippers were used to cover up footprints of the kurdaitcha raiding party. Others insist that karara were worn to strike terror in the hearts of enemies. One glimpse of the distinctive feather marks in the dust was enough to cause the aborigines to avoid the spot—the same way someone from another culture might stay away from a place said to be haunted by a ghost. Who knew where kurdaitcha might strike next?

Karara *of western Australia were carefully made of emu feathers and human hair.*

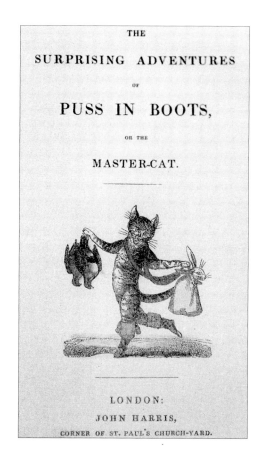

THE

SURPRISING ADVENTURES

OF

PUSS IN BOOTS,

OR THE

MASTER-CAT.

LONDON:
JOHN HARRIS,
CORNER OF ST. PAUL'S CHURCH-YARD.

This children's book published in England in the early nineteenth century, The Surprising Adventures of Puss in Boots, *has ancient roots in Italy.*

Countless fairy tales feature shoes as a magical means of escape. "Puss in Boots" and "Seven-League Boots" include powerful footwear that helps heroes make marvelous journeys to seek their fortunes. Fairy tale shoes are used to trick devils, witches, and robbers. Some shoes are danced to pieces; others drop coins with every step. On occasion shoes are rewards. Heroes receive blue glass boots that help them scale mountains; wanderers win iron shoes that never wear out. Fairy tales abound with poison slippers, fur slippers, stolen slippers. There

are slippers worn by swan maidens, by dogs, by simple-
tons and braggarts.

Where would Cinderella be without her slippers? One
of the most popular of all fairy tales, "Cinderella" exists
in more than 300 versions from countries around the
world. The most ancient Cinderella was recorded in
Egypt more than 2,000 years ago, though the heroine is
named Rhodope, and her shoe is a delicate golden sandal.

Perrault retold Cinderella
*with dark, mysterious
illustrations by Gustave
Doré in 1850.*

A ninth-century Chinese Cinderella features a tiny gold slipper. In Vietnam the slipper is embroidered. The first time the familiar glass slipper appeared in the printed English version of "Cinderella" wasn't until 1697, when the story, written by Charles Perrault, was translated from the French. The English editors made a mistake. They thought the French word *vair* (a kind of white fur called miniver) was a misprint for *verre* (glass). In the English translation, Cinderella's slipper became fragile, unstretchable glass—more magical than ever.

"The Worn-out Dancing Shoes" by two German brothers, Jacob Grimm (1785–1863) and Wilhelm Grimm (1786–1859), tells what happens to twelve dancing princesses. Every night they are locked in their room by their tyrannical father. Every morning their dancing slippers are worn away with holes. How do they escape? Their father is determined to find out. In some fairy tales, shoes are not just careless evidence—they're deadly. Danish writer Hans Christian Andersen (1805–75) was the son of a poor shoemaker. In his story "The Red Shoes," scarlet slippers dance the main character to death.

*T*his 150-year-old leather shoe has a cracked wooden sole. The heel is lopsided with wear. A hole gapes on one side. The mate is missing, probably never to be found again. Although this shoe doesn't look promising, it was once considered very powerful.

Where will this shoe take you?

Back to where it was hidden for more than a century—inside the wall of a cottage in Stanwick, Northamptonshire, England. This old shoe, which may have originally belonged to a young girl, was purposefully bricked inside the cottage wall to serve as a good luck charm to protect the house and all who lived there. The shoe was not discovered until the cottage was torn down in 1969.

Informal records kept by one shoe expert for the past fifteen years have shown that more than 700 such old shoes have been discovered inside walls, under roofs and floors, and tucked away near chimneys in Britain, Belgium, France, Germany, Spain, Switzerland, Finland, and the rest of Scandinavia—not to mention Turkey, Australia, Canada, and America. Some are nearly 600 years old. Others are less than seventy. Single, worn shoes are most often discovered. Sometimes they are accompanied by another shoe or

Girl's brown leather shoe from 1700, hidden for years inside a wall.

perhaps personal objects—an old spoon, a glove, a tobacco pipe.

At Papillon Hall in Leicestershire, England, the deed was written so that no future owner would ever be able to remove from the dining room wall a pair of brocaded shoes. The shoes had once belonged to the daughter of the house, who died in the eighteenth century. Why did the grieving relatives put the shoes in the mansion wall? Perhaps because they simply could not bear to throw them away.

The present owners of Papillon Hall would do well to follow the deed's advice. One British family reportedly removed a concealed shoe from the wall of their house to send it to the Museum of London for identification. Immediately, the house became haunted. Only when the shoe was replaced in its rightful spot did the haunting stop.

What is the origin of concealing shoes in house walls? No one knows for sure. One clue might be the fifteenth-century legend of a parish priest of North Marston in Buckinghamshire named John Schorn. This English clergyman became one of England's "unofficial" saints for creating an unusual miracle. He could "conjure the devil into a boot."

Long ago, shoes and boots may have been considered effective traps for catching evil spirits. This theory may explain why so many hidden shoes are discovered inside chimneys and near windows—points of entry that homeowners would most wish to protect. It also helps to unscramble the reason so many outlines of shoes and boots have been discovered scratched on the lead roofs of churches.

Like many doting parents, the mother and father of Belgium's King Leopold II saved his first shoes, which were made of cerise pink silk and kept inside a wooden box with a note proudly marking his birthdate: April 9, 1835.

Chapter 7

Shoes and Life's Milestones

Birth, Death, and Marriage

> Hoping this night my true love to see
> I place my shoes in the form of a T.
> —ANONYMOUS ENGLISH SAYING

Elinor Pruitt Stewart never owned a pair of shoes until she was six years old. Born in 1876, she spent most of her luckless childhood in Oklahoma Territory caring for eight orphaned brothers and sisters. When she was thirty-three years old, she answered a Wyoming rancher's ad in the *Denver Post* for a housekeeper and went west. After what she called "a powerfully short engagement," she agreed to marry her employer, a soft-spoken Scottish widower. "We had to chink in the wedding," she wrote, "between planting the oats and other work."

*Satin wedding slippers
from the nineteenth century.*

There was no time to sew a wedding dress, but she did manage to ride horseback many miles to the nearest town to buy one important item to celebrate her new happiness—"a beautiful pair of shoes." The stylish high-button satin boots were glorious, even though they were a bit too small. "[M]y vanity had squeezed my feet a little," she admitted.

A spring blizzard blew in from the mountains on her wedding day. She was so "topsy turvy" cooking and cleaning, she didn't have time to change into her fashionable wedding shoes before the guests arrived and the ceremony began. "Happening to glance down," she wrote, "I saw that I had forgotten to take off my apron or my old shoes, but just then Mr. Pearson pronounced us man and wife, and as I had dinner to serve right away I had no time to worry over my odd toilet."

Whatever happened to Elinor's wedding shoes? She undoubtedly found a good use for them. Any ranch woman who could milk seven cows twice a day, cut hay, cook three meals a day for a threshing crew, and put up thirty pints of gooseberry jelly was not someone who would allow "even the smallest thing to go to waste"— including stylish wedding shoes.

In different countries around the world, shoes help celebrate important milestones in people's lives—from courtship to marriage, from birth to death.

Ancient Greeks didn't mail valentines to express their devotion. They carved their beloved's name on the soles of their sandals. Wherever they walked, the names were imprinted in the dust. In the fifteenth century in Europe, a man who wanted to show a woman he wished to marry her presented her with a jug in the shape of a pointed beak shoe that was engraved with the words "I want no one else."

Why a shoe? Ask Johann Wolfgang von Goethe (1749–1832). He wrote to his lover, Christine Vulpius: "Please send me your last pair of shoes, worn out with dancing, as you mentioned in your letter, so that I might

According to an old, popular superstition, the young man who trod on his wife's foot ensured his authority over her. Note the pointed shoes, or crackows.

have something to press against my heart."

Shoes have been handy for catching glimpses of future husbands or wives. Among Moroccans, it is believed that if a man finds a slipper in the road, he'll soon find a wife. An old English custom says that young girls will find out who they'll marry on Midsummer Eve if they carefully arrange their shoes by their bedsides and chant:

Point your shoes toward the street,
Leave your garters on your feet, put your stocking on your head,
And you'll dream of the man you're going to wed.

In 1860, there was tremendous commotion in a small Leicestershire village when the father of the bride suddenly hurled a battered hobnailed boot, which he had found in the road, right over the departing bridal carriage. Had he lost his mind? No. He was simply following an ancient good luck ritual for newlyweds.

As soon as the boot crashed into the rhododendrons, shrieking bridesmaids still wearing their finery plunged into the hedge. Each was intent on grabbing the old boot

A father hands the bride-groom his daughter's shoe to symbolize the transfer of authority in the painting by Abraham Bosse called Wedding Night *(1633).*

first to be assured of being the next to marry. Once found, the dirty boot was taken inside the house and hung from a white satin ribbon—a symbol of good luck and the wish for many children.

The custom continues today. Instead of tossing old shoes, groomsmen simply tie worn footwear to the back of the car of the bride and groom before they drive away. In China, red bridal shoes are thrown on the roof of the house to ensure happiness and to make sure everyone knows that the newlyweds are enjoying their honeymoon.

Traditional Hindu weddings in India often include the *mehndi* ritual. On the night before the ceremony the bride's sisters paint lacy designs on the soles of her feet with henna. The dye, which at first appears green, turns red—a lucky color—when the bride washes her feet the next morning. Some brides double their good fortune by also wearing special hammered silver sandals. In the northwest African country of Morocco, new slippers, sent by the bridegroom, are placed on the bride (who has had her feet painted with henna). A silver coin is placed in the bride's right slipper for good luck. This custom is echoed in England. Many years after Lucia Pickering married John Wheatland in 1923, her family gave her wedding outfit to a museum. The donation included a fancy gown and shoes with jeweled buckles—complete with the lucky coin still tucked inside!

Old Woman in the Shoe

*I*n mountainous areas of China, childless women wishing to have a son or daughter carried beautifully embroidered doll-size shoes called *manitijiren sha* and placed them on holy shrines. Women in Lancashire, England, who hoped to become pregnant tried on the shoes of a woman who had just had a baby.

The link between shoes and babies may help explain the origin of the familiar nursery rhyme below.

Some historians believe that the old woman who lived in a shoe was based on Queen Caroline of England (1683–1737) who had eight children and was married to George II (1683–1760). Other historians insist that the rhyme had its origin in Colonial America, where it was inspired by Elizabeth Vergoose of Boston who reportedly had ten stepchildren plus six of her own—a total of sixteen. Quite a crowd!

The Old Woman In The Shoe

There was an old woman
who lived in a shoe,
She had so many children
she didn't know
what to do;
She gave them some broth
without any bread;
She whipped them all
soundly and put them to bed.

Shoes are utilized as symbols in deaths and funerals. In funeral processions for American presidents, a riderless horse is marched at the head with one backward boot in its stirrup to represent the fallen leader. Among the Ashanti of West Africa, it is customary for mourning tribesmen to paint their sandals black when a king dies.

During the Victorian era a century ago, shoes served

Aristocratic Korean men wore these white kajukshin, *or leather shoes, to funerals.*

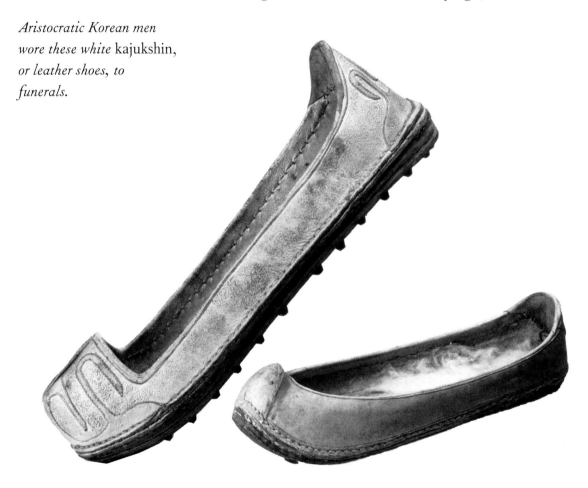

Where Will This Shoe Take You?

as mementos after a death, especially an untimely death of a child. These sentiments are best expressed in a poem clipped from a nineteenth-century newspaper that was found tucked inside a tiny red leather shoe donated to the Essex Institute in Massachusetts:

> *I found it here—a worn-out shoe,*
> *All mildewed with time and wet with dew*
> *'Tis a little thing; ye would pass it by*
> *With never a thought, or word, or sigh:*
> *Yet it stirs in my spirit a hidden well,*
> *And in eloquent tones of the past doth tell.*

This miniature shoe is two and one-half inches long and four inches high—just big enough for a doll. It is made of finely woven cotton decorated with tiny square silver plates, and the shoe sole was carefully made of silver.

If you could fit into such an amazing boot, where would it take you?

To the high, dry Chancay valley on the north coast of Peru. More than 1,000 years ago, this was the home of a powerful civilization that had developed irrigation systems for crops, erected pyramids, and built enormous walled cities with straight roads and orderly city blocks. Chimu artisans created amazing pottery, textiles, and metalwork with silver and gold. Unfortunately, no written language developed to record the daily life of these mysterious people. Much of what we know about the Chimu has been uncovered from well-preserved grave sites.

This miniature silver boot was found in the ancient grave of a child in Peru. Other objects found there included a feather crown, miniature musical instruments, a silver tree, shell-bead slings, bracelets, and bags.

This silver-plated boot was discovered in 1968 by archaeologists. Accompanying the boot were all kinds of other personal objects. Historians think that the Chimu provided the dead person with not only food and weapons but all his favorite possessions to make afterlife as agreeable as possible.

While noblemen might have been buried with tiny silver slippers like these, working-class Chimu men were buried with their fishing lines and hooks; working-class women were buried with spindles, distaffs, and sewing workbaskets. Next to the corpses of children were terra-cotta dolls. Sometimes mummified pets—dogs and parrots—were found buried with their masters.

Was this silver boot a good luck symbol? Perhaps. To early Peruvians, silver represented the tears of the moon. It was considered a noble, elegant metal. Chimu craftsmen were experts at mixing silver with copper, then hammering it into molds, embossing or engraving it in many different ways. One Renaissance artist from Germany, Albrecht Dürer (1471–1528), was so moved when he saw silverwork taken from a similar Chimu grave, he wrote, "I have seen the things which were brought from the new golden land . . . all fairer to see than marvels."

A professional ballerina may dance her way through sixty-five pairs of toe shoes per month.

Chapter 8

Shoes and Play

From "Croquet Sandals" to Air Jordans

> *I wear a different pair of shoes every night. It's funny because when I explain why I do that, everyone can relate. . . . You feel energized, you feel a little better about yourself. That's why I started doing it. I didn't do that my first year. But as I started putting on a new pair of shoes I felt like, "I'm walking out there with my own shoes and I'm happy as hell."*
>
> —MICHAEL JORDAN, CHICAGO BULLS
> *MICHAEL ON MICHAEL*

Every day you probably walk an average of 10,000 steps. This translates into nearly 500 tons of pressure for each of your feet. A basketball player like Michael Jordan may make as many as 10,000 steps—and absorb a total of more than 1,000 tons of pressure in his feet—in one game alone. When a ballet dancer who weighs 100 pounds lands after performing a grand jeté, nearly a quarter ton of pressure slams into her feet, and yet she keeps dancing. No wonder Italian inventor and artist Leonardo da Vinci (1452–1519) declared that the human foot with its 26 bones, 19 muscles, and 106 liga-

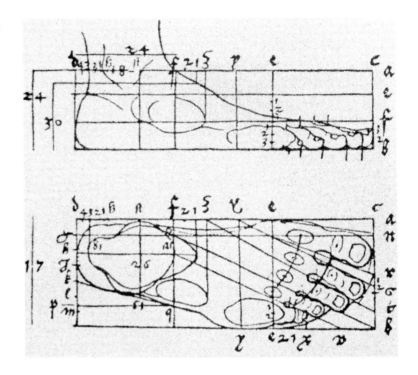

ments is a "masterpiece of engineering and a work of art."

Amazingly enough, comfortable, affordable shoes designed for athletic activity have been available in the United States only since the turn of the century. One of the technological breakthroughs that helped make this possible came about through the sheer grit and determination of an American inventor named Charles Goodyear (1800–60).

For almost twenty years, Goodyear had been fascinated by the possibilities of a curious substance known as india rubber. Imported from the tropics, where it was harvested from trees, rubber had amazing properties. It bounced. It was waterproof, elastic, lightweight, durable.

The problem was that in hot summer temperatures rubber became soft and sticky. (Imagine wearing rubber suspenders and suddenly losing your pants because your body temperature caused the rubber to sag!) In winter rubber turned iron hard. (When the first waterproof rubber coats were introduced in 1823, they rattled like sheet tin; the folds could not be pried apart.) The first rubber-soled shoes fared no better when they were first sold in 1832. Who wanted footwear that stuck to the floor in summer or turned as brittle as bricks when winter came?

Goodyear spent decades studying the properties of rubber. Eventually, he invented a heating process called vulcanization that transformed rubber into a tough, dependable material. In 1844 he applied for a U.S. patent and began trying to raise money to manufacture and promote improved rubber products—everything from rubber dishes and rubber bands ("useful and convenient for druggists and tradesmen") to rubber pistol holsters, life preservers, ship sails, and carriage tires. He invented tieless rubber shoes for children, waterproof boots, and rubber "chair shoes" guaranteed to prevent noise and carpet wear. Rubber, he wrote, was one of the best nonconductors of electricity. "[A] person having on India rubber shoes [sitting on a rubber chair or laying in a rubber bed] need have little apprehension of danger from lightning."

Unfortunately, less honest businessmen than Goodyear stole his vulcanization idea, used Goodyear's name, and made a fortune. When Goodyear died in 1860, he was largely unknown and deep in debt. Meanwhile, rubber making had grown into a multimillion-dollar business in America. Shoemaking was revolutionized by improved rubber soles and new machines that could punch

The twentieth century in America heralded the first commercial shoe stores where customers could purchase ready-made shoes produced in factories in a variety of sizes.

holes in soles and uppers; split, roll, strip, and cut sole leather; crimp boot uppers, and attach the heel with pegs—faster than any human hand.

In 1868, canvas uppers and laces were added to rubber soles, creating more comfortable "croquet sandals," the first true sport shoe designed for playing the lawn game croquet. However, the new rubber-soled shoes cost six dollars, too much for anyone except the very rich. In 1873, croquet sandals were renamed "sneakers." By the turn of the century, Sears Roebuck Catalogue had begun listing factory-made rubber-soled shoes for only sixty cents a pair. Seventeen years later, U.S. Rubber introduced Keds (named from a combination of the words "kids" — the target audience — and "ped" — Latin for foot). This basic sneaker remained in style for fifty years.

In the 1940s, due to raw material shortages caused by World War II, synthetic rubber began to be manufactured on a large scale in the United States. Approximately 70 percent of all rubber (natural and synthetic) was used for making tires. A large proportion of the rest was used to create footwear.

In 1972, a University of Oregon track coach named Bill Bowerman was struggling to find a better way for runners to get traction from lightweight shoes that didn't need metal spikes. Inspired one morning by the pattern in an open waffle iron, he decided that square spikes were the answer. Excited by his design, he poured liquid urethane into the waffle iron, closed it, and let it cook.

Legend says that he opened it and there was the waffle sole of a new athletic shoe. (What really happened was that the waffle iron bonded shut because he had forgotten an important ingredient in the urethane formula.)

He tried the experiment again with another waffle iron and came up with the first signature shoe of a new company named Nike, named after the Greek goddess of victory. Designers added a wedged heel, cushioned midsole, and nylon tops and created the first true running shoe.

Nike's fortune bloomed in 1984 when the company signed basketball superstar Michael Jordan as spokesman for Air Jordan shoes with ad campaigns such as "It's Gotta Be the Shoes." Nike sold nearly 100 million pairs

The Nike Waffle Trainer was introduced in 1974 with a unique outsole.

Michael Jordan of the Chicago Bulls became a Nike spokesperson in 1984.

shoes in 1992 and again in 1993—about 200 pairs every minute.

Interestingly enough, 90 percent of people who buy athletic shoes purchase them for casual wear, not athletic activity. Perhaps fashion cycles repeat themselves more than we realize. Just as Englishmen in the nineteenth

Recent Nike Air Jordan designs, developed since Chicago Bulls basketball star Michael Jordan endorsed the first Nike Air Jordan court shoes in 1985 when he was a rookie.

century were criticized for constantly wearing boots when they had no intention of riding horses, Americans today wear athletic shoes although they have no intention of playing basketball or running a marathon. Comfort, easy fit, and relatively low cost have contributed to this shoe's popularity. As a result, more than 360 million pairs of rubber-soled athletic shoes (representing more than $11 billion in business) were sold in the United States in 1994 alone.

Even an enthusiast like Goodyear would undoubtedly be amazed.

Shoes from the Outfield to the Ski Slope

"We had only twelve men on the roster. I was first off a pitcher, but when I wasn't pitching I played in the outfield. I played in a brand new pair of shoes one day and they wore blisters on my feet . . . I tried [playing] with my old shoes on just couldn't make it. [The manager] told me to play anyway, so I threw away the shoes and went to the outfield in my stockinged feet. I hadn't put out much until the seventh inning. I hit a long triple and I turned it on. The bleachers were close to the baselines there. As I pulled into third some big guy stood up and hollered.

"You shoeless sonofagun you!"

"They picked it up and started calling me Shoeless Joe all around the league, and it stuck."

—JOSEPH JEFFERSON JACKSON, "SHOELESS JOE,"
LEGENDARY MEMBER OF THE 1919 CHICAGO BLACK SOX
SHOELESS JOE AND RAGTIME BASEBALL

Advances in polyurethane injection molding have helped create lightweight, durable ski boots.

Golf shoes make use of the oxford design with a differ-ence—spikes.

Lightweight, comfortable hiking boots are often seen on city streets—not just mountain paths.

Skateboarding takes sports shoes to new heights.

Bowling shoes provide special traction surface.

Where Will This Shoe Take You?

$\mathcal{L}$ace your left foot inside this worn blue Adidas running shoe. Where will it take you?

To Canada in 1980 during an amazing cross-country journey called the Marathon of Hope.

The shoe belonged to Terry Fox, a twenty-two-year-old Canadian, who ran with an artificial limb more than halfway

This navy-blue nylon Adidas running shoe experienced miles of wear while it was worn by Terry Fox during his heroic Marathon of Hope in 1980.

across the country—nearly 3,339 miles—to raise money for cancer research. "I'm not a dreamer," he said, "and I'm not saying that this will initiate any kind of definitive answer or cure . . . but I believe in miracles. I have to."

Fox, the son of a Canadian National Railway switchman, grew up in Vancouver, British Columbia. He was the second of four children. All his life he enjoyed sports. Like most teenagers, he spent most of his time wearing athletic shoes. In high school he played varsity basketball and ran cross-country. In 1977, the year he entered college, Fox complained of pain in his leg. Doctors made a devastating discovery—bone cancer. Fox's right leg was amputated. He was fitted with an artificial limb that could be used with a normal shoe. For the next eighteen months, he underwent grueling chemotherapy.

Other people might have given up. Not Fox. He decided to make a transcontinental run to help raise funds for cancer research. "I was determined," he said, "to take myself to the limit for the cause."

On April 12, 1980, he dipped his artificial leg and blue running shoe into the Atlantic Ocean at St. John's, Newfoundland, and began the marathon run to Vancouver. He planned to run thirty miles a day until he reached the Pacific Ocean, following a route that would take him through as many towns as possible. The shoes he wore were remarkably simple by today's high-tech standards for athletic shoes. Nothing fancy—just a rubber sole and nylon upper. "He'd step with his left leg," one observer recalled, "then twist his whole body to throw his artificial leg ahead of him. It was sort of a step, hop and skip."

At first, few people understood what he was trying to do. Little by little, the crowds grew, impressed by his courage, hope, and determination. For the next four and a half months, newspapers, magazines, and television covered his day-by-day trek. Terry Fox became a hero—not only in Canada but around the world.

On September 1 in Thunder Bay, Ontario, Terry Fox was forced to stop running because of breathing difficulties and chest pains. The bone cancer had spread to his lungs. On June 23, 1981, one month short of his twenty-third birthday, he died.

Although Terry Fox never finished the marathon, he reached his goal. He helped raise $20 million for cancer research—more than any other single effort in the Canadian Cancer Society's history.

In memory of his valiant effort, Fox's running shoe was eventually sold during a celebrity auction to raise further cancer research funds. The Canadian Cancer Society later donated the shoe to the Bata Museum Foundation in Toronto.

Terry Fox did more than help in the struggle to find a cure for cancer. He changed people's attitudes. As one Canadian writer observed, "He showed that cancer, however brutally it treats the cringing flesh, can't defeat the spirit."

A six-year-old Austrian orphan has just received his first new pair of shoes as part of the post-war relief effort of the American Red Cross.

Conclusion

". . . look for me under your bootsoles."

—WALT WHITMAN
"SONG OF MYSELF"

"You cannot put the same shoe on every foot," wrote Publilius Syrus, a Syrian-born writer living in Rome. Although he recorded these words more than 2,000 years ago, his advice still holds true today.

Lucky for us.

There are many shoes, many stories. From around the world, individual sandals, boots, oxfords, pumps, clogs, mules, and moccasins provide fascinating glimpses into different cultures and environments—if we take the time to look carefully, sleuth diligently, and allow our imaginations to soar.

Credits

Invaluable footwear, photograph, and art collections were made available through the Scholl College of Podiatric Medicine, the Field Museum of Natural History and the Art Institute in Chicago; the Metropolitan Museum of Art and the American Museum of Natural History in New York; the Bata Shoe Museum in Toronto; the Library of Congress and the Ford Theatre National Historic Site in Washington, D.C.; the Northampton Borough Council Central Museum in England; and the Greenland National Museum and Archives in Greenland.

Page

vi   From the Wisconsin State Historical Society, Madison.

x   "Footwear Sayings" by Aimee Liu and Meg Rottman from *Shoe Time* © 1986 by Aimee Liu and Meg Rottman, p. 43. Used by permission of William Morrow, Inc.

xii   From the Field Museum, neg. 13219, Chicago.

4   From Redfern, *Royal and Historic Gloves and Shoes*, p. 107.

5   From Scholl College of Podiatric Medicine.

6   From Otis, *Primitive Travel*, p. 368.

7   From *National Geographic*, 1908, p. 657.

Page

9   From Gardiner, Sir Alan, *Egyptian Grammar*, Oxford, England: Ashmolean Museum, Griffith Institute, 1927, p. 5.

11   From the Metropolitan Museum of Art, neg. 98370, New York.

12   From Frobenius, Leo, *Rock Painting*, NY: Museum of Modern Art, 1937, p. 35.

13   From the Greenland National Museum and Archives.

14   From Frobenius, Leo, *Rock Painting*, NY: Museum of Modern Art, 1937, p. 51.

15   From *The Art of the Stone Age*, p. 77.

Annotated Bibliography

Because so many of the books in English on costume and footwear have a Eurocentric slant, the job of uncovering global information required dedicated sleuthing. Another challenge was the breadth of time covered: nearly 100,000 years. A helpful starting point was provided by "The Foot and Shoe: A Bibliography," by Charles Collazzo Jr. (Toronto: Bata Shoe Museum Foundation, 1988), a comprehensive listing that includes oral history accounts on early shoemaking.

Relevant sources are listed by chapter in the order in which they were used. If a source appears more than once, subsequent listings include only the title.

Introduction

A Home in the Woods: Pioneer Life in Indiana, Oliver Johnson's reminiscences of Early Marion County as related by Howard Johnson (Bloomington, IN: Indiana University Press, 1991).

"The Speaking Shoe" by Nancy Rexford *(Essex Institute Historical Collections*, April 1991). Analyzes how best to use shoe artifacts to investigate history.

Shoe Time by Aimee Liu and Meg Rottman (NY: Arbor House, 1986). Facts and stories about shoes told in a lively manner.

Chapter 1: The First Shoes

Primitive Travel and Transportation by Otis Tufton Mason (Washington, DC: Government Printing Office, 1896). Excellent scholarly article analyzing development of footwear.

Human Odyssey by Ian Tattersall (NY: Prentice Hall, 1993). Illustrated overview of migration and lifestyle of early humans.

"Peopling the Earth," (*National Geographic*, Vol. 174, No. 4, 1988). Examination of how and where earliest humans migrated.

The Human Dawn by the editors of Time-Life Books (Alexandria, VA: Time-Life Books, 1990). Examination of theories of evolution with examination of early archeological finds.

"Moccasins and Their Relation to Arctic Footwear" by Gudmund Hatt (*Memoirs of the American Anthropological Association*, Vol. III, 1916). Thorough interpretation of the development of moccasins.

Pride of the Indian Wardrobe by Judy Thompson (Toronto: Bata Shoe Museum Foundation, 1990). Maps and photos enhance descriptions of northern Athapaskan footwear.

Athapaskan Women by Julie Cruikshank (Ottawa: National Museum of Canada, 1979). Oral accounts reveal early customs, traditions, and moccasin construction.

On Snowshoes to the Barren Grounds by Caspar Whitney (NY: Harper and Brothers, 1896). Early account of white encounters with Inuit.

Athapaskan Clothing (*Fieldiana Anthropology*, NS No. 14) by James W. VanStone (Chicago: Field Museum of Natural History, 1981). Detailed examination of clothing and footwear.

Painting, Sculpture and Architecture of Ancient Egypt by Wolfhart Westendorf (NY: Harry B. Abrams, 1968). Illustrated volume features early Egyptian art, including Narmer palette.

Treasures of Tutankhamen (Metropolitan Museum of Art) edited by K. Gilbert and Joan Holt (NY: Ballantine Books, 1976). Color photos highlight statues, textiles, and footwear.

Howard Carter and the Discovery of the Tomb of Tutankhamen by H.V.F. Winstone (London: Constable and Co. Ltd., 1991). Includes fascinating first person account of Carter's discovery.

Egyptian Grammar (third edition) by Sir Alan Gardiner (Oxford, England: Griffith Institute, Ashmolean Museum, 1927). Early Egyptian symbols described and usage highlighted.

Masterpieces of Egyptian Art by Hermann Ranke (London: Allen and Unwin, 1951). Photos enhance descriptions of statues and murals depicting early footwear.

The Development of Footwear by the editors of the Society of Chemical Industry in Basel, Switzerland (Vol. 34, June 1940). Excellent art references show the development of shoe styles.

The Mode in Footwear by R. Turner Wilcox (New York: Charles Scribner and Sons, 1948). Shoe sketches accompany text.

The Ancient World by Giovanni Garbini (NY: McGraw-Hill, 1966). Cave paintings from around the world highlighted in photos.

Let There Be Clothes by Lynn Schnurnberger

(NY: Workman Publishers, 1991). Humorous examination of footwear and costume.

Twenty Thousand Years of Fashion: The History of Costume and Personal Adornment by Francois Boucher (NY: Harry B. Abrams: 1967). Illustrations provide background for earliest to latest fads.

The Art of the Stone Age: 40,000 Years of Rock Art by Hans-Georg Bandi (London: Methuen, 1961). Spanish cave paintings.

Prehistoric Rock Pictures by Leo Frobenius (NY: Museum of Modern Art, 1937). Original cave art rendered in drawings.

"World of Ancient Ice Man Comes into Focus" by Brenda Fowler (*New York Times*, June 21, 1994). Shows Ice Man clothing.

"The Ice Man: Lone Voyager from the Copper Age" by David Roberts (*National Geographic*, June 1993). In-depth account of the discovery and analysis of Ice Man, including footwear.

The Greenland Mummies by Jorgen Meldgaard and Jorgen Nordquist (Washington, DC: Smithsonian Institute, 1991). Detailed exploration of early Arctic clothing and footwear.

Greenland Then and Now by Erik Erngaard (Copenhagen: Lademan, 1972). Overview of Greenland climate, land, and way of life.

"Arctic Skin Clothing in Eurasia and America: an Ethnographic Study" by Gudmund Hatt (*Arctic Anthropology*, Vol. V, No. 1, 1969). Translates Danish theory on footwear adaptation.

Chapter 2: Shoes and Protection

Cavalry by John Ellis (NY: G.P. Putnam, 1978). Excellent analysis of use of the horse by soldiers around the world.

Man and the Horse edited by Diana Vreeland (NY: Simon and Schuster, 1984). Includes development of stirrup and riding boot.

Art of Ancient Mesopotamia by Anton Moortgat (NY: Phaidon, 1967). Photos highlight architecture, sculpture, and murals.

The Mode in Footwear.

"Moccasins and Their Relation to Arctic Footwear."

The Greenland Mummies.

"Clogs or Wooden Soled Shoes" by Evelyn Vigeon (Costume: *Journal of the Costume Society*, No. 11, 1977). Delightful examination of the making and wearing of wooden-soled shoes and clogs.

Christmas the World Over by Daniel Foley (Philadelphia: Chilton Books, 1963). Describes St. Nick's customs.

Texas Boots by Sharon De Lano (NY: Viking Press, 1981). How earliest cowboy boots came to be, plus modern equivalents.

"Bruce Collection of Eskimo Material Culture from Port Clarence, Alaska" by James W. VanStone, Vol. 67 (*Fieldiana Anthropology*, 1967). In-depth look at clothes, footwear, and socks.

The Development of Footwear.

Shoes: Fashion and Fantasy by Colin McDowell (NY: Rizzoli, 1989). Whimsical look at shoes through the ages.

The Mode in Footwear.

The Sex Life of the Foot and Shoe by William M. Rossi (NY: Saturday Review Press, 1976).

Overview of shoe history, plus detailed examination of Chinese footbinding customs.

Arctic Research and Life Among the Esquimaux by C.F. Hall (NY: Harper and Brothers, 1896). Actual account of early explorer's encounter with Inuit.

"Moccasins and Their Relation to Arctic Footwear."

Chapter 3: Shoes and Authority

The Invention of Tradition edited by Eric Hobsbawn and Terence Ranger, (Cambridge, England: Cambridge University Press, 1992). Essays include discussion of colonial India "shoe wars."

The Fabrication of Louis XIV by Peter Burke (New Haven, CT: Yale University Press, 1992). How Louis XIV "invented" image with costume, footwear, and public ceremony.

The Development of Footwear.

The Mode in Footwear.

Costumes of the Classical World by Marion Sichel (NY: Batsford, 1980). Illustrated reference of costume and footwear.

Thomas Jefferson: A Biography in his Own Words by the editors of Newsweek Books (NY: Newsweek, 1974). Actual documents reveal Jefferson's personal life and career.

Two Centuries of Costume in America by Alice Morse Earle (Williamstown, MA: 1974). In-depth description of costume and footwear in colonial America and beyond.

All About Shoes: Footwear Through the Ages (Toronto: Bata Shoe Museum Foundation, 1994).

Full-color, multicultural examination of shoes from around the world.

Cyclopaedia of Costume or Dictionary of Dress (2 volumes) by James Robinson Planche (London: Chatto and Windus, 1879). Early illustrated look at origin of costume and footwear.

Lincoln by Philip B. Kunhardt, Jr., Philip B. Kunhardt III and Peter W. Kunhardt (NY: Alfred Knopf, 1992). Oversize book with many photos captures spirit of Lincoln.

"How Big Was Lincoln's Toe?" by Gabor S. Boritt, speech presented February 12, 1989 at the 57th Annual Lincoln Dinner, Redlands, CA.

Chapter 4: Shoes and Status

Twenty Thousand Years of Fashion: The History of Costume and Personal Adornment.

The Mode in Footwear.

Guinness Book of Records by the editors of Facts on File (NY:Facts on File, 1994). Source for most expensive shoes on record.

"Everybody's Business, Nobody's Business," by Daniel Defoe (*A Journal of the Plague Year and Other Pieces*, Garden City, NJ: Doubleday, Doran and Co., 1935.) Describes status of rural girl in 1725 based on dress.

Shoes by June Swann (Somerset, England: Butler and Tanner, Ltd., 1982). Highlights footwear history in England.

Working Dress in Colonial and Revolutionary America by Peter F. Copeland (Westport, CT: Greenwood Press, 1977). Delightful sketches illustrate common people, middle class, and upper class.

African-American Adornment: A Cultural Perspective by Barbara M. Starke (Dubuque, Iowa: Kendall Hunt Publishers, 1990.) Includes oral history accounts of slavery conditions.

Chaucer's World edited by Clair Olson and Martin Crow (NY: Columbia University Press, 1948). Actual words in documents of period.

The Age of Indiscretion by Clyde Davis (Philadelphia: Lippincott, 1950). Humorous reminiscence of growing up in a small, Midwestern town at the turn of the century.

The Development of Footwear.

Early American Dress by E. Warwick (NY: Benjamin Blom, 1965). Sketches help bring to life the costumes of the colonial period.

The Common Man Through the Centuries by Max Barsis (NY: Frederick Ungar Pub. Co., 1973). Sketches provide glimpse of costume and footwear of common people.

Two Centuries of Costume in America.

Royal and Historic Gloves and Shoes by W.B. Redfern (London: Methuen and Co., 1904). Footwear photos; includes commentary.

Let There Be Clothes.

A History of Shoe Fashion by Eunice Wilson (NY: Theater Art Books, 1968). Thorough examination of European footwear styles.

Customs and Superstitions of Tibetans by Marion Herbert Duncan (London: Miter Press, 1964). Highlights Tibetan beliefs and describes clothing and footwear of different classes.

Indians of the Plains by Robert H. Lowrie (Lincoln, NE: University of Nebraska Press, 1982). Informative overview of customs and way of life of the Native Americans of the Plains.

Let There Be Clothes.

The Sex Life of the Foot and Shoe.

Things Chinese by J. Dyer Ball (Hong Kong: Kelly and Walsh, Ltd., 1903). Early observations of Chinese dress and customs.

"How the World Is Shod," (*National Geographic Magazine*, Sept. 1908, Vol. XIX, No. 9). Includes turn-of-the-century photos.

Godey's Lady's Book and Magazine (Philadelphia: Louis A. Godey, 1830–1898). Leading nineteenth-century magazine mirrors women's fashions and societal status.

"The Speaking Shoe."

Elizabethan Pageantry by H. K. Morse (London: Studio, 1934). Beautifully illustrated book captures art and observations of the time.

Chapter 5: Shoes and Fashion

A History of Shoe Fashion.

Modes and Manners (4 volumes) by Max Von Boehn (NY: J.B. Lippincott Co., 1932). Extensive costume, footwear illustration, and origin with illustration from periods shown.

Shoes by June Swann (Somerset, England: Butler and Tanner, Ltd., 1982). Insightful discussion of development of English footwear with color photos.

The Development of Footwear.

Visual History of the Sixteenth Century by Jane Ashelford (NY: Batsford, 1963). Fascinating glimpse of costume and fashion, especially of upper class.

Shoes: Fashion and Fantasy.

Accessories of Dress by Katherine Lester (Peoria, IL: Chas. A. Bennett Co., 1954). In-depth description of footwear through the ages with European emphasis.

Early American Dress.

Royal and Historic Gloves and Shoes.

The Mode in Footwear.

Everyday Life in Traditional Japan by C. J. Dunn (NY: G. P. Putnam, 1969). Glimpse into early footwear and costume.

Japanese Costume by Helen Benton Minnich (Tokyo: Tuttle, 1963). Beautiful book highlights Japanese traditional dress.

The Mode in Footwear.

History of Costume by Blanche Payne (NY: Harper and Row, 1965). Extensive overview of clothing and footwear through the ages.

Chapter 6: Shoes and Magic

The Wonderful Wizard of Oz by L. Frank Baum (NY: Dover Publishing, 1900). Original classic.

The Wizard of Oz and Who He Was by M. Gardner (East Lansing, MI: Michigan State University Press, 1957). Insights into the creation of Oz.

The World of Oz by Ellen Eyles (Tuscon, AZ: HP Books, 1985). Helpful biographical data on Baum and how he wrote the book.

"The Significance of Cinderella and Her Slipper" by Lisabeth M. Holloway (*The ClioPedic Items*, Vol. 2, No. 2). Analysis of Cinderella story across cultural lines.

All the French Fairy Tales by Charles Perrault (NY: Didier, 1946). Includes illustrations by Gustave Doré.

A Treasury of Illustrated Children's Books by Leonard De Vries (NY: Abbeville Press, 1989). Full-color, oversize book contains early chapbooks.

The Mode in Footwear.

Eighty Fairy Tales by Hans Christian Andersen (NY: Pantheon Books, 1976). Translated from the original Danish, with illustrations.

Complete Fairy Tales of Brothers Grimm, translated by Jack Zipes (NY: Bantam: 1987). Original stories from the German.

Folklore and Customs of Rural England by Margaret Baker (London: David Charles, 1974). Entertaining discussion of rural beliefs and superstitions.

Archeology of Ritual and Magic by Ralph Merrifield (London: B.T. Batsford, 1987). Excellent look at shoes in customs.

Northampton Museum and Art Gallery Journal (6) by June Swann (London: Northampton Museum, 1969). Global study of hidden shoes.

Australian Aborigines by A. Elkin (Sydney, Australia: Angus and Robertson, 1938). Helpful guide to early ritual study.

Native Tribes of Central Australia by Baldwin Spencer (London: Macmillan, 1899). Revenge ritual described in depth.

Australian Aborigines: How to Understand Them by A. P. Elkin (London: Angers and Robinson, 1938). Early observation of way of life of Aborigines.

Feather Arts: Beauty, Wealth and Spirit from Five Continents by Phyllis Rabineau (Chicago: Field Museum of Natural History, 1980). Illustrated book highlights feather artwork, including karara from Australia.

O the Times! O the Manners! by William Iversen (NY: Wm. Morrow and Co., 1965). Humorous examination of customs.

Ritual and Belief in Morocco, Vol. 1 and 2 by E. Westermarck (London: Macmillan, 1926). Highlights north African beliefs and superstitions.

"Rossi's Believe It or Not," by William A. Rossi (*FNM* April 1988). Global overview of shoe customs and healing powers.

Pride of the Indian Wardrobe.

Springs of Mende Belief and Conduct by W. T. Harris and Harry Sawyer (Freetown: Sierra Leone University Press, 1968). Discussion of African customs and footwear beliefs.

The Romance of the Shoe by Thomas Wright (London: C. J. Farncombe and Sons, 1922). Includes early shoemaking information, myths, customs, and superstitions.

Put Your Foot Down by Florence E. Ledger (Melksham, Wiltshire, England: C. Venton, 1985). Shoe history told with anecdotes.

Chapter 7: Shoes and Life's Milestones

Letters of a Woman Homesteader by Elinore Pruitt Stewart (Boston: Houghton Mifflin Co., 1913). Delightful correspondence of nineteenth-century Montana farm woman.

Shoes: Fashion and Fantasy.

The Romance of the Shoe.

Ritual and Belief in Morocco.

Folklore and Customs of Rural England.

Notes and Queries, Serial 4, Vol. 2 (London: G. Bell, 1868). Includes anecdotes about English wedding customs involving shoes.

Costumes and Featherwork of the Lords of Chimor by Anne Pollard Rowe (Washington, DC: Textile Museum, 1984). Illustrated book reveals the beauty of Peruvian burial artifacts.

Notes of Julie Jones, curator of pre-Columbian art, Metropolitan Museum of Art, NY.

PreInca Art and Culture by H. Leichet (NY: Orion Press, 1960). Overview of climate and social setting of Chimor.

Desert Kingdoms of Peru by Victor W. VonHagen (Greenwich, CT: NY Graphic Society Publishing, 1964). In-depth description of early civilization, with theories about burial items' meanings.

The Mode in Footwear.

Everyday Life in Early India by Michael Edwards (London: Batsford, 1969). Follows individual throughout day in early India, providing insights into clothing, way of life.

"The Speaking Shoe."

All About Shoes.

Fieldiana, Part II, Vol. XXVI, Pub. 396 by Paul S. Martin (Chicago: Field Museum). African customs involving shoes.

"The Speaking Shoe."

"Children's Shoes in the Thirteenth to Sixteenth Centuries," by Margaret de Neergaard (*Journal of the Costume Society*, No. 18–19, 1984–85). Lively discussion of archeological find in England.

Mongol Costumes by Harold Hansen Henny (Copenhagen: Carlsberg Foundation, 1993). Color illustrations and photos enhance this book about clothing and footwear.

The Real Personages of Mother Goose by Katherine Elwes Thomas (NY: Lothrop, Lee and Shepard Co., 1930). Early attempt to verify historically characters from Mother Goose rhymes.

Oxford Nursery Rhyme Book by Iona and Peter Opie (Oxford, England: University Press, 1955). Classic collection of early chapbook rhymes and children's books.

Chapter 8: Shoes and Play

Rare Air: Michael on Michael by Michael Jordan (San Francisco: Collins Publishers, 1993). Oversized, illustrated life and career story told by Jordan.

All About Shoes.

The Shoe Show: British Shoes Since 1790 edited by Ken and Kate Baynes (London:Crafts Council, 1979). Excellent book detailing English footwear and shoemaking.

India Rubber Man: The Story of Charles Goodyear by Ralph F. Wolf (Caldwell, ID: Caxton, 1939). Readable biography of inventor's life.

Rubber's Goodyear: The Story of a Man's Perseverance by Adolph Regli (NY: J. Messner, 1946.) Discussion of invention of rubber, highlighting Goodyear's sacrifice.

Accessories of Dress.

Shoes: Fashion and Fantasy.

The Development of Footwear.

Swoosh: The Story of Nike by L. Becklund (NY: Harcourt, 1991). Fascinating history of sport-shoe company's rise.

Michael Jordan edited by Dr. James Beckett, (NY: House of Collectibles, 1995). Jordan's career from baseball to basketball.

"Terry Fox, Canadian Hero Dies," by Henry Giniger (*New York Times*, June 19, 1981).

"He is More than You Can See," by June Callahood (*MacLean's*, September 15, 1980).

"Marathon Man of Hope" by Warren Gerard (*MacLean's*, July 6, 1992).

All About Shoes.

Sales statistics provided by Athletic Footwear Association, North Palm Beach, Florida.

Shoeless Joe and Ragtime Baseball by Harvey Frommer (Dallas, TX: Taylor Publishing Co., 1992). Includes actual testimony by Shoeless Joe during Chicago Black Sox trial.

Conclusion

Portable Walt Whitman edited by Mark Van Doren (NY: Penguin Books, 1945). Excellent reference to nineteenth-century American poet.

Index